FADED INTO TRUTH

Poetic Essays
and Stories
of a
Barbershop Griot

FREEZY THE BARBER

WASHINGTON
AVENUE
PRESS

ISBN: 979-8-9996644-2-6
Library of Congress Control Number: 2025921078
First Edition

Cover & Interior Design: James A. Freeman
Published by Washington Avenue Press
Printed in the United States of America

This is a work of poetic essays. Names, characters, places, and
events may be the product of the author's imagination or used in
a literary context. Any resemblance to actual persons, living or
dead, is purely coincidental.

Dedication

For my mother, Alma Mae Mack — "Big Alma" —
the spine of my art and the lavender thread running
through every page.

For the barbers who came before me, the silent
teachers whose hands and hustle shaped the shop into
a classroom.

For the barbering community, past and present, that
raised me inside its four walls and taught me how to
pass the craft forward with intention.

For my clients — soldiers, students, fathers, sons,
daughters — who have trusted me with their crowns
and their stories, whether for a single cut or for years
at a time. Thank you for letting me preserve your
dignity, share your milestones, and give my own pain a
place to land while I stood behind the chair.

And For the future barbers — the students in schools,
the kids with clippers in their hands and dreams in
their heads. Keep listening. Keep learning. Keep
observing. Think bigger than the four walls of the
shop. Everything you soak up now will shape you
later. Bring back, and carry forward, the dignity and
integrity of the barbershop.

This book is for all of you.

TABLE OF CONTENTS

THE SHOP AS A STAGE: *Barbershop Chronicles*

CURVE BALLS & CLIPPERS ~ *When the Lines Blur*

The Shop That Built Me

There's a rhythm in a barbershop that can't be taught.

The hum of clippers. The faint smell of alcohol and talc. The way sunlight hits the mirror just right as a man looks at himself, deciding if he approves.

A shop isn't just a place for haircuts, it's a confessional, a comedy club, a war room, a sanctuary.

I was fourteen when I started cutting. I didn't know then that this chair would teach me more about life than any classroom or lecture hall. In this shop, I've been both a student and a mentor.

I learned about love and loss, betrayal and brotherhood, laughter and pain. I watched boys become men. I saw men crumble and triumph in the same day. I've been a barber, a mentor, a referee, a counselor, and sometimes, just a silent witness.

We mastered a kind of mental math in the shop. The quiet calculations barbers make when a guy comes in on Tuesday with a swollen right hand, talking about how he "handled his business," and on

Wednesday, another walks in with a busted left eye, swearing he "fell down the stairs." We put two and two together. We know the story, but we keep our mouths shut. A raised eyebrow, a smirk, a nod that's all it takes to say, "We know." Because a barber's loyalty is in silence as much as in skill.

This book is a collection of those moments not just fades and lineups, but stories. Some raw, some hilarious, some heavy enough to settle on your chest like a weight. They're stories of people I've met, lessons I've learned, and truths I couldn't have seen coming. They're not just about me, they're about us.

The barbershop is a griot's corner. These are the tales it whispered into my clippers' motor.

The Chair is Sacred

The lavender spine was my mother's touch, soft and proud on the back of my book. I handed it to him, this quiet client—not my favorite, but familiar enough. He held it without ceremony and said, "That's cool," in that monotone voice. Still, I spoke of her—my mom—how she nurtured my gift of art, how I knew she'd be proud of me. Then I paused, breathed in the silence, and let out what had been pressing against my chest: "I really miss my mom."

Not thirty seconds later, he scoffed at a text. "My mom don't even say hi. Just sends YouTube videos. Next time, I'ma block her ass." I flinched inside; that shift felt sharp. But it wasn't anger, not really. It was something else. A line slipped out before I could weigh it: "I wish I had that problem."

And then, like a pin in my chest, he said, "You can't wish for somebody who doesn't love you." I froze and said the only thing I could: "I understand." I didn't. Not then. But I understood enough to let him be.

I didn't correct him, didn't try to wrap my love around his lack, didn't say, "You shouldn't talk about your moms like that."

Because the truth is, people grieve the living all the time. But the world only understands one kind. Grief over death is clean—cut and dry. People know what to say, when to say it. They bring flowers, wear black, and make space. But grieving what you don't have in someone is a lonelier grief. There are no funerals for unmet needs, no sympathy for emotional starvation, just silence and shame.

I lost my mom to death. He lost his to neglect, to silence, to emotional starvation. Both are losses. One just comes with flowers. The other, confusion. And in that moment, I realized: true empathy isn't about shared experience, it's about shared space. "I understand" doesn't always mean "I've lived it." Sometimes it means, "You're safe here."

The barber chair is sacred—not just for fades and lineups, but for invisible battles made briefly visible. Sometimes, a client lets one slip, and when they do,

I don't swat it down. I let it land. That's what makes this more than a cut.

That's how I became a griot—a witness not just to hair, but to humanity. I didn't just have a moment; I held it, learned from it, and now I can teach it. Because sometimes, what heals a man isn't what you say. It's what you don't.

Author's Note

When Painting With Words arrived on my doorstep, still warm from the press, Oz came through for a cut and flipped through the pages like a proud cousin, grinning, "You gotta sign mine!" It felt good to see my work in his hands. Minutes after he left, another client walked in—a man I'd cut before but who never gave off the warmest energy. Socially awkward and hard to read, we had made small talk about cars over the months, and he knew I'd been working on a book. So while my clippers hummed, I showed him the finished copy. He nodded politely, then noticed the lavender spine. "That purple's pretty cool," he said. "It's for my mom," I told him. "Lavender was her favorite color. She was the spine of my art." The words rolled out before I could stop them. "She'd be proud of me. I really miss her."

Seconds later he scoffed at a text from his own mother. Something about her had annoyed him. In that moment the cut went quiet.

I combed, he stared at his phone, and a small conviction settled over me. Here I was, a 44-year-old barber who'd been holding clippers since fourteen, still learning new lessons in my own chair. At fourteen, grief might've made me lash out. At forty-four, it made me listen. I finished his cut without preaching. As he stood to leave I simply said, "Hope things get better with you and your mom, man." He paused, met my eyes, and said "Yeah." It was the first real thing he'd said the whole appointment.

Two days later a message popped up on my phone—a video of him drifting his car at night, neon tires cutting circles through the dark. "Looks dope at night, right?" he wrote. It was his way of saying thank you. Since then, he's shown me more of his world, pulling me outside to admire his car, sharing small pieces of himself.

That quiet exchange became the opening of this book. It reminded me that even after thirty years behind the chair, I'm still a student of the shop—still learning patience, still learning how quickly a moment of empathy can soften a hard shell, and still grateful that the chair—my chair—keeps teaching me

Fresh Fade (in the Front)

"Beginnings are like fresh fades—awkward at first but already holding the shape. With each pass of the blade, skill meets vision, and what starts rough becomes a cut that tells its own story."
—*Freezy the Barber*

Before the shop, before the barber chair, it started in our little Bronx bathroom—a chair wedged in front of the sink, mirror fogged with ambition. We called it "The Beach." I'd dip fingers into Blue Magic grease, carve ocean waves across Chink's head with nothing but a skinny comb and a steady hand, like I was sketching coastlines. Josh got the same treatment—a front-row seat to my experiments, trusting me with his crown long before I'd earned anyone's trust.

Then came the face trimmers, the battery-powered kind made to chase stubble, not shape destinies. But I lined up foreheads and temples like they were royalty. Eventually, somebody's forgotten clippers landed in my hands—cheap house clippers, plastic guards rattling like maracas. And that's when I graduated to fades.

Chink was my first masterpiece. At least, that's what I thought. He left the house feeling fresh, waves gleaming, line sharp, the kind of cut that made heads turn. In class, heads did turn.

Compliments rained down, kids impressed because he wasn't rocking the usual even-all-over Caesar. He had a fade. A real one. Sort of.

Duval—seventh-grade detective with a stutter sharp enough to cut deeper than my clippers—blurted out from the back of the class, "Wh-who the fff-fff messed up your h-hair like that?" His eyes locked on Chink's neckline, where my skills had abandoned me.

Turns out, the fade was only fresh in the front. The back was a crime scene: harsh lines, dark patches, a baby afro tuft sticking out like a witness in hiding. By the time Chink got home, he'd already solved the problem—took it all down to a clean Caesar. No evidence remained.

But that embarrassment lit a fire. I obsessed over the back of heads, memorized every blend I saw at the shop, peppered real barbers with questions. Fade lines became my algebra, clipper work my geometry, hair my canvas. Failure sharpened me like the steel I gripped in my hands.

—.

Josh became my next canvas, rocking thick zigzag parts an inch wide, like roadmaps carved into his crown. He loved them. We thought we were fly. Looking back, we looked crazy—but crazy was the price of practice.

Those bathroom sessions were our laboratory, our studio, our thought bubble. Two younger brothers as guinea pigs, trusting me with their image before the world trusted me with theirs.

That's where I fell in love with this craft—before money, before clout, before being called "the GOAT." Back when a "shop" was a chair, a mirror, and my little brothers laughing at the results. I didn't know it then, but those botched fades and bold parts were the blueprint of my future. The bathroom was my barber school. Failure was my first teacher. And my brothers were my first clients—and my first believers.

First believers, first victims. They wore every mistake like a badge until I got nice. But yo… I really used to mess my brothers' heads up. Damn.

The First Five Dollars

~And the words that came with it

Five dollars fades fast, but a kind word plants belief that lasts.

Mo Better Cuts, Harlem. Mr. Hoover gave me my first real shot and even loaned me the money for a pair of T-Outliners. My first client wasn't a fade or a lineup; it was a shave. A middle-aged brother with a thick mustache and scruffy cheeks — more than a five o'clock shadow but not quite a beard.

He didn't want a full haircut or a shape-up. Maybe that's why he gave me a chance. I was nervous but steady; all I had to do was clean him up with clippers. Five dollars for a clipper shave. My first five dollars as a barber. I think he gave me six, but back then five was a lot. I wish I would've kept that bill as a trophy.

I remember the sound of the blade crunching through his sandpaper-thick stubble. No hot towel, no razor yet — just me, clippers, and a stranger's face. My chair was on the new side of the shop, where they were knocking out walls to build a salon. Separate entrance, separate vibe, first chair in an empty room.

When I told him he was my first customer, he rubbed his face in the mirror and said, "And it was a good one." Those words went further than the five dollars. Thirty years later I still remember his face, the feel of the clippers, and the quiet thought in my head: You're in business now. The world is watching.

Mr. Hoover

Dreams live in your head until someone gives them a chair — Mr. Hoover gave me mine.

It started at Mo' Better Cuts on 135th and Lenox, Harlem, 1995. I was just a kid from the Bronx, a church choir boy cutting heads in hallways and kitchens, but I walked into that shop one day and said it plain: "I want to be a barber."

Inside were men who carried the craft with pride. Gary with the sharp, silent eyes, laser-focused on every line he carved. Kool-Aid, who could fill the shop with a laugh and still lay down a fade that stopped traffic. And Mr. Hoover, stoic, sharp-dressed, the kind of man whose handshake felt like a signed contract. That place smelled like years of work — aftershave, clipper oil, and the faint sweetness of hair burning off a straight razor. It was a time capsule, a bridge back to when barbershops were more than businesses; they were temples of manhood.

I came back every day. Sat on the benches, watched, studied every flick of a wrist, every pass of the comb. It was like barber school without tuition.

Eventually, I brought my nephew in — a test, a chance to prove what my hands could do. I cut him with a pair of cheap Sports Clippers, thin-wired, not built for real work. But I made him clean, and the shop noticed.

Mr. Hoover pulled me aside. "You're good, kid," he said. He loaned me $43.27 so I could walk out with my first pair of Andis T-Outliners. It wasn't just a loan; it was belief. I worked that debt off cut by cut, then saved enough for a pair of Wahl Super Tapers. The day I bought those clippers, I felt like I'd been handed a sword.

I became the kid in the shop sweeping floors, passing out flyers, cutting heads under Harlem's watchful eyes. At fourteen, I was making my own money, learning responsibility, earning respect. On my 17th birthday, Mr. Hoover handed me a surprise: an apprentice license application, fresh from the library printer. He gave me three dollars for a passport photo and told me how to get my TB test done. Two weeks later, my picture was laminated on a license hanging above my station.

That man didn't just help me get a job — he made me a barber. That shop became my classroom, and those men became my professors. Gary's precision, Kool-Aid's confidence, Mr. Hoover's quiet guidance — those lessons are in every fade I've ever done.

I don't know if Mr. Hoover's still alive. Back then he was already a legend, gray around the temples, wisdom etched deep in his face. But if this reaches him somehow, I want him to know: the GOAT I became started with his faith in a fourteen-year-old kid. And I've carried that torch into every cut, every shop I've built, every barber I've mentored.

Because he gave me more than a chair. He gave me a future so thank you Mr. Hoover.

I used to walk past Mr. Hoover's shop on 131st Street after choir practice, peeking in like it was a classroom. One day he gave me more than a view—he gave me a chance. That chair became my first real station, and his quiet faith turned a teenager with clippers into a lifelong barber carrying his lessons in every fade I've ever done.

The Blowout That Blew

Out of Proportion"

~The day I made a proud Nigerian man cry

Every master cut begins as a mistake. My first blowout turned into a crisis, but it was also my initiation— sweat, humility, and one steady hand willing to pull me from the deep water. Those early stumbles didn't break me; they built the griot I am now.

Every tear rolling off his strong Nigerian face matched a bead of sweat sliding down my forehead. Between us, we created a river deep enough to hydrate the driest parts of Africa. Mo didn't just walk over to help me; he limped over like a lifeguard of the barbershop sea, coming to rescue a drowning rookie with a trembling clipper.

It was Saturday at Cuts Galore, also known as New Africa—a packed Bronx barbershop buzzing with energy, laughter, and competition. Ten barbers lined up like gladiators, all chairs full, every set of clippers singing its own tune. And there I was, the youngest, a 14year-old with the least clientele, finally cutting hair with the rest of the men, finally feeling like I belonged. But what I was doing to this man's head was a crime.

It was my first blowout, and I didn't know the science yet. I picked his hair out, shaped it, then—mistake. Picked it out again, shaved some more, again and again. Each time I combed it out, it got shorter, more uneven, like I was carving potholes into a once-proud crown. This wasn't just a haircut; it was the slow collapse of a man's dignity. And I watched as this large, proud African brother—a man who probably grew up herding goats, carrying water, and surviving things, I can't even imagine—sat in my chair with tears in his eyes. Ancestors looking down on him in shame seeing their son's spirit being broken by a 16 year old kid.

He kept shifting, adjusting himself in silence, holding back anger but unable to hide the pain. Every tear he dropped, a nervous bead of sweat slid off my forehead. Together we were filling a river. That's when Moe Dread, the soft-spoken legend with one leg and more skill than anyone I knew, stood up from his chair. Mo was an amputee, his prosthetic leg giving him a signature limp, but his walk had authority. He saw enough. He swam—I mean came over, calm, collected, with the kind of respect that makes you love your mentors.

"Lemme see that" he said, and the barbershop turned its attention to us.

Moe took the clippers, narrating like a teacher, guiding my trembling hands.

"This is how you sculpt, smooth it out, keep the rhythm," he murmured, moving hand-over-hand with me. Piece by piece, he brought the disaster under control. The haircut was shorter now—much shorter than what the man came in for—but Moe shaped it into a crown again. The man finally spoke, his Nigerian accent thick with pain and pride:

"I'm never coming back to this place."

I wanted to sink through the floor. The entire shop saw it. But I didn't quit. I couldn't. Because this is what paying dues looks like. Humiliation in front of your peers, sweat dripping like rain, and the realization that your heroes are watching—not just your failures, but your response to them.

Those days in Cuts Galore were an education like no other. Doob, Nay, Boo Black (rest in peace), Derrick, Byo, Nazz, Mike, and Mo—they were the gods of the fade. Artists, teachers, warriors with clippers. I was the kid sweeping hair, cleaning clippers, sitting in silence while the shop roared with grown-man conversations. And yet, these men brought me up. They let me take chances. They corrected me without malice. They molded me into what I am today.

When I look back, I realize that moment was my initiation. If paying dues was a person, it was me: a kid in a Bronx barbershop on a Saturday, drowning in sweat while my first blowout turned into a haircut emergency. And now? That same kid is a GOAT. That same nervous rookie is a master barber, a griot, a teacher to others.

I'll never forget Moe limping over to save me, not because of the haircut, but because of the way he carried himself—steady, patient, humble. He didn't clown me. He built me. That's the thing about barbering: every legend is carved out of mistakes. Some tears, some sweat, a whole lot of humility—and one man willing to limp across the room and pull you out of deep water.

Lessons on 3rd and Claremont

~ Piecing Together a Curriculum

I never went to barber school; I came up through apprenticeship. By the time I landed at Cuts Galore — now New Africa — on 3rd Avenue, I had my apprentice license and a hunger to learn everything. Up the block on Claremont sat Mr. Emilio's shop, a Puerto Rican barbershop with the feel of an old Italian salon. Emilio was a classy man — slicked-back silver hair, pressed shirts, always neat.

In the Bronx back then, barbershops were friendly but still segregated. Black barbers cut mostly coarse hair, Puerto Rican barbers cut finer hair. Music, language, technique — everything had its own rhythm. But I wasn't interested in boundaries. I wanted every skill, every technique.

Most of us Black barbers didn't use straight razors then. Our skin wasn't raised on daily razor shaves, and apprenticeship didn't teach it. But I knew the state board would, and I wanted to be ready. So on my breaks I'd walk out of my shop and into Emilio's. He never treated me like an intruder. He saw a young kid who wanted to learn and he said yes.

He sent me down to the local discount store, Dollarite, to buy balloons and a pack of Wilkinson Sword blades. He showed me how to break the double-edge blades in half, load them into a straight razor, and hold it with pinky and fingertip like a violin bow. "If you pop the balloon, you cut the client," he said. "Keep a forty-five-degree angle, go with the grain."

I never popped a balloon. Fear kept my hand steady — like opening a tube of Pillsbury biscuits, waiting for the pop but never letting it happen. Those lessons built my confidence and set me apart. I became the young guy who actually used a razor, who could blend fine hair like coarse hair, who was willing to leave his own shop to study at another.

That's still me. Whether it's writing books, building a publishing company, or learning a new skill, I take everything the extra mile. Why not? Mr. Emilio's balloon never popped, and neither has my drive.

The Early Bird Gets to Learn

I used to joke that the early bird gets the worm, but in my case the early bird got the wisdom. Back in my foundational years I didn't have a line of clients waiting yet, so I spent my mornings on the other side of the shop, learning from the ladies.

I was raised by women, taught by women, and in the shop it was no different. Vanessa and Nuncie were older than me, around my sisters' ages, and they'd be in early prepping their stations. My sisters would come hang out with them too. I'd watch, I'd ask, and I'd learn.

I never earned a beautician's license, but I learned how to wash hair, prep clients, even do weaves. I wasn't ashamed of it either. People laughed and found it abnormal, but I knew the truth: most folks who mock vision are the ones who don't have one.

Those mornings gave me skills that still matter. I've done my daughter's hair, my grown daughter's hair, and I still do my seven-year-old's hair sometimes.

Learning from women taught me more than technique — it taught me how to be a man. Cooking, cleaning, respect, chivalry, honesty… the elders and godmothers and teachers in my life showed me all of that.

So when dudes cracked jokes about me blending a weave, I just smiled. The baddest chicks on the block were coming to me, not them. I was straight, I was confident, and I was building skills that broke old gender barriers. Those women, from the neighborhood to the beauty shop, were my first teachers. They taught me how to conduct myself as a man long before I ever had a full book of clients.

Keys to the Next Level

*Sometimes a set of keys isn't just for opening doors—
it's the first glimpse of the room you're meant to build.
Every shop has its first kid—the one who reminds you
that someone younger is always watching.*

By 2000 I'd already bounced through a few shops, always carrying my livelihood in a bag. Clippers, guards, brush — I lived out of that bag the way some people live out of a suitcase. Sometimes it really was my suitcase; I'd slept in my car before. But wherever I went, I could eat because I could cut.

That winter I was nineteen, a young father with a one-year-old daughter, Dominae, tagging along in her stroller. Up on Boston Road, across from Crotona Park, I walked past a place called International Barbershop. No barber in sight, just a Ghanaian owner named Charles with a thick accent and an empty chair. "I need a barber bad," he said. No audition, no license check. Just come.

Within days we were running a $5 holiday special. The money helped me buy gifts for my daughter — I always went big for Christmas, even broke. The shop had a beauty-salon side too, so my sister Dawn braided hair there for a while.

Toya and Yolanda, who became like family to me, worked there too.

I didn't just cut hair; I curated the vibe. Charles worked full-time elsewhere, so he gave me the keys. I opened and closed the shop, collected commission, kept the place safe enough to bring my baby girl. No thugs, no rowdiness, just a young barber running a clean, quiet shop on Boston Road.

For the first time I was the best barber in the room. My razor skills were sharp, my confidence high. The shop was only as good as I was, and I made sure to be as good as I could be. Looking back, International Barbershop was more than a gig. It was my rite of passage — the winter I stopped being a kid in someone else's shop and became a man leading my own chair.

T-Rex

Every shop has its first kid—the one who reminds you that someone younger is always watching.

When we first opened up our shop, a skinny seven-year-old Puerto Rican boy walked in with a serious look in his eye and a buck-toothed smile. "My name is Carlos," he said, "but you have to call me T-Rex." From that moment on nobody in the shop ever called him Carlos again.

He lived upstairs with his single mother and baby sister, Destiny, whom we affectionately called Princess. His mom barely spoke English but worked hard to hold her family together. T-Rex was only seven but already looking for work — sweeping floors, running errands, anything to ease his mother's load. He didn't come to cut hair; he came to carry responsibility.

I admired that. I'd been raised by strong women too. I knew what it meant to grow up fast. We gave him small tasks and a safe place to hang out after school. He'd sit at the chessboard or the table, do his homework, sweep between cuts, translate for his mom.

He was also the reason we started our report card program. At first it was just an excuse to put a little money in his pocket. Any kid who brought in a report card with an 80 average or better got a free haircut, and the ten-dollar fee went straight to the student. Before long we were giving out cuts and cash to a whole crew of kids, but it started with T-Rex.

Years later he found me on Facebook. The profile said "Carlitos Ramirez," but all I saw was "T-Rex." He'd grown into a fine young man, striving for the Air Force, still reaching out to ask my advice.

Looking back, T-Rex was my first real chance to give back — not just cutting hair but helping a boy who was trying to be the man of his family. He reminded me that no matter where you are in life, someone younger is watching. I was still finding my own way, but through him I started to understand what it meant to lead and to serve. Barbering showed me that precision isn't just in the hands, it's in the heart."

Shaping Myself in Someone Else's Memories

A single gesture may fade from your day but live forever in the memory of another.

We weren't just cutting hair. Even back then we were trying to cut through the distrust.

There was a lady who worked with food banks and somehow managed to funnel donations our way even though we were a for-profit shop. She'd drop off turkeys, canned goods, boxes of food. We'd chip in some of our own money too.

On Thanksgiving week we went around the corner to the shelter, starting at the top floor and knocking on every door. T-Rex was with us, a couple of the other kids too. Some moms were skeptical — life had taught them to expect a catch. But when they realised it was real, the whole mood shifted.

You'd see a five- or seven-year-old peeking from behind a door, a kid who'd already resigned himself to "no dinner this year," and then watch his eyes light up at the sight of a frozen turkey and a bag of food. We didn't just fill a fridge; we rewrote a memory.

Both of us had grown up with single mothers, poor but proud.

We knew what it felt like to smell everyone else's cooking and have nothing. Mr. T's Meat Market had been me and my brothers' first taste of hustling for Thanksgiving meals — passing out circulars together, carrying boxes upstairs, working for the food itself. Nay's mom, an immigrant from Haiti, raised her kids the same way. That's why the giving back hit so deep: we were shaping the memory we wished someone had shaped for us.

It probably meant more to me than to them. But that's what a barbershop can be at its best — two men, a couple of kids, and a hallway full of doors, trying to replace "we had nothing" with "we got blessed."

The Milk Carton

If she'd walked into the wrong shop that day, she might've ended up on a milk carton. That was the Bronx for you — a city where a teenager from Connecticut could vanish in a heartbeat. But she didn't walk into the wrong shop. She walked into ours.

It was one of those brutal Bronx winter days, wind slicing like razors, and she stepped in wearing open-toed sandals — feet red, stiff, and numb. She was a kid, sixteen, chasing some dude she'd met on a chat line. The kind of story that starts with a bad idea and could've ended in tragedy.

Instead, she asked to use our bathroom. We let her. She disappeared for a while, and we started clowning. "Yo, she's in there murdering the bathroom," my boy joked, and I imagined the soundtrack: Let the bodies hit the floor! We were laughing, but there was a seriousness under it. We knew where she was. We knew what could happen if she'd stepped into a different shop.

When she finally came out, we got to talking. She was young, but she wasn't dumb — just naïve, soft-spoken, and clearly relieved to be around people who cared. She told us the guy never showed. She was stuck in a city she didn't know, in the middle of winter, with nobody looking out for her but strangers.

So we became that. We teased her about those sandals, sang a remix of Linkin Park's "Numb" just for her: My toes become so numb, I can't feel my feet... She cracked up. And instead of running back to the train, she stayed all day. We kept the jokes going, but we also made sure she was safe. By the time we closed the shop, she'd thawed out, and we'd made a friend for life.

Lauren is grown now — mid-30s, a musician, a woman with her own stories and wisdom. But we still laugh about that day, about how reckless she was, and how that moment could've gone left if she'd trusted the wrong barbershop. Because not every shop is a sanctuary. But ours was.

Over the years, other girls came through too, kids really — high schoolers helping us pass out flyers, hanging out just to feel safe, venting about boyfriends while we gave their dudes the firm handshake and What's your deal, man? stare. We became big brothers, uncles, mentors without the title. They grew up, moved on, some became parents, some designers, some just stayed in touch. But none of them ended up on a milk carton.

Because that's the kind of shop we ran. We could've been grimy like other spots, but we weren't. We built a place where even a scared white girl from Connecticut in open-toed sandals could walk in off the street and feel safe.

And that's what barbering really is: not just fades and lineups, but being a pillar. Being a guardian. Being a witness. The kind of man who makes sure your story doesn't end in tragedy.

That winter evening with the sandals girl wasn't just a random moment; it was the point where our shop stopped being simply a place to get a haircut and started becoming a heartbeat. From then on we weren't only shaping hairlines — we were shaping people's days, their sense of safety, their memories. Those early years were our apprenticeship in community-building as much as in barbering.

The Chess Vendetta

Before this story is about chess, it's about Adam.

My brother-in-law who's really been more like a brother—present since I was eleven, still here at forty-four. In a life where most men drifted, Adam stayed. He worked hard, drove buses, raised a family, and showed us, quietly, that you can hold down your post year after year. He wasn't a father figure, but he was a living example of a man who keeps showing up.

And he's funny. The guy roots for the Mets and every other team destined to break his heart. He'll take an "L" in stride, then stay up half the night practicing so he can win next time. He's the underdog's underdog— and somehow he makes losing hilarious.

One day, after countless losses to Nay, Adam came into the shop with a look in his eye. He didn't just want to play; he wanted revenge. He'd studied, prepared, and that day he finally got his win.

This piece isn't just about a chess match. It's about a man who's been around for three-quarters of my life, whose persistence and patience taught me as much as his humor did.

My brother-in-law Adam — bus operator, New York City Transit, twenty years in — was always a competitive man. Football, Madden, chess — you name it. He hated losing with a passion.

When I say hated, I mean he would lose a game of Madden to my boy Shannon and then stay up half the night sketching plays like he was Bill Parcells, just to come back the next day with new strategies. I think he finally beat Shannon once, and then he quit while he was ahead.

Chess was no different. In the shop, Adam always went up against Nay, and Nay had his number. Every time, Adam would be this close, and then it would slip. He'd slap his knee, "Damn, that was the move right there. I saw it too late." He'd walk away muttering, replaying the board in his head like it was a film session.

One afternoon, he came through on break from the depot at West Farms and Tremont, uniform still on, the look in his eye different. He wasn't coming for a cut.

He wasn't coming to hang out. He was coming for blood.

"Yo Nay, set the board up. I came here to beat you today."

The whole shop perked up — barbers on pause, clients leaning in, a couple of us just shooting the breeze in the corner. Adam planted himself at the chair like it was a heavyweight title fight. And somehow, after all those close calls and near-misses, he did it. He beat Nay.

He stood up, grinned like he'd just won the Super Bowl, and said, "I'm good now." And that was it. He walked out the shop, hopped back on his bus route, and never played Nay again.

Adam came in with a vendetta, settled his score, and left undefeated — in his own book at least. That was classic Adam.

Mental Math

Silence can solve equations louder than words ever will.

In the shop we called it "mental math." Not algebra, not geometry — just putting two and two together. A man walks in on Monday with a swollen right hand, bragging about how he "handled his business." On Wednesday another man limps in with a swollen left eye, swearing he "fell down the stairs." Me and Nay exchange that silent look across the shop: we already solved the equation.

But you'll never hear us say it out loud. That's the code. Barbers have ears to the street but mouths shut. We hear it all — breakups, beefs, promotions, secrets — and we keep it all where it belongs. In our heads. It's not our job to announce what we know; sometimes it's our job to protect people from what they don't.

I've even used "mental math" to keep somebody safe. If I knew one client had vowed to knock out another and saw both of them heading toward the same corner, I'd slide in a quiet warning. "Yo, traffic's crazy over there — take the long way." "They blocked off the street."

"You might wanna swing around West." It sounds casual, but the eyes say: trust me, go the other way.

Nobody knows I intervened. Nobody can accuse me of taking sides. But more than once that little detour probably saved somebody from an ass-whipping, a charge, or worse.

That's the real math of a barber. We take all the numbers we're given — swollen hands, swollen eyes, rumors, tempers — and add them up without blowing up the equation. We mind our business, protect the vibe, and let men walk out with a clean cut and maybe, quietly, a clean slate.

Because in the barbershop, knowing it all isn't power. Knowing it all and staying silent — that's wisdom.

Where's the Money?

A barber can build four walls, sweep every corner, and still never know what kind of storm will blow in. The real craft isn't just the cut — it's how you clear the air without cutting anyone down.

Every shop has its characters. Ours had a customer —
cool as hell but clearly living rough — the kind of guy
you like but don't trust with extra cash. He was always
trying to give me a little "hold this for me" money, but
I never accepted it. In the barbershop world, a favor
from a man like that usually comes with a hook in it.

Most weeks he'd bargain for a cut. But one day he
came in with cash in hand, no haggling, no hesitation.
Sat down in Nay's chair looking like he'd hit the lotto.
Everything felt off.

Halfway through the cut the door opened and in
walked a burly woman with two tall teenage sons. She
gave me a polite smile when I greeted her but then
stood by the entrance, hands clasped, eyes locked on
the chair. Her sons stood behind her like quiet
enforcers.

When Nay spun the chair, our customer looked like
he'd seen a ghost. "Where's the money, D?" she said.
"What money? Don't come in here with no bullshit,"
he sputtered.

"You went in my house," she fired back, "and you stole my money out of my dresser drawer. And then you came here. Where's my money?"

The sons shifted forward, ready to handle it. They weren't bad boys; you could see they were only there to protect their mom's honor. But it was about to go sideways fast.

I stepped in. Calm voice, steady eyes. "Ma'am, I don't know what went on between you two, but this is our place of business. We can't have this kind of thing happening here." I spoke to the boys too, reminding them they didn't want to catch a charge for somebody else's mess. Slowly the heat drained out of the room. She stayed respectful to me, and eventually she and her sons left without incident.

Once the door closed, me and Nay lit into our man. "Bro, don't bring that kind of drama into our shop. Whatever dirt you're doing, do it somewhere else."

He denied it, of course, but he heard us. Later he'd talk about trying to get clean. Over time he came back with little bits of good news about his life.

That day reminded me why I eventually moved to a private suite. A barbershop is neutral ground, but it's also a magnet for all kinds of energy. One bad moment can drag everyone into the crossfire. As a barber you're not just cutting hair — you're managing people, defusing tension, and trying to keep the integrity of the space alive.

Even in a sanctuary, chaos can find a seat. The barber's job is to keep the peace steady while the work is done.

The Mad Muslim

The barbershop has always been a hub for hood entrepreneurs. At Cuts Galore — New Africa — one of ours was a hustler we nicknamed the Mad Muslim. He was like a walking contradiction: part street peddler, part Nation of Islam preacher, part Canal Street wholesaler. You could hear the jailhouse-Nation cadence in his voice, like a sermon about bean pies that somehow turned into a pitch for socks and body oil.

He never came in like a normal salesman. No "Good morning, brothers, would you like to see…?" He'd wait until the shop was packed, then march down the line dropping bottles, oils, socks — whatever he had — right on each station like you'd already bought it. By the time you picked it up to read the label he'd be halfway down the row, hustling the next chair.

And if you hesitated? He'd wheel back around, voice rising, fingertips pressed together like an Italian chef explaining a secret recipe: "Why you acting like that? You got everybody looking at me like my product is…" (pause) "…Garbage."

He said "garbage" like it was capital-G Garbage, like a Million Man March speaker delivering a prophecy. Then he'd snatch the bottle back off your station, give us that slow, stomping exit and disappear until the next week with a fresh batch of "deals."

We never knew his real name. To us he was always the Mad Muslim, hustling socks and oils with a felonious preacher's flair. Half the time we didn't buy a thing; half the time we actually needed what he was selling. But every time he walked in, the shop stopped cutting and started laughing — and that's how he earned his place in the legend of New Africa.

Garnishment,

~Not Through Court, But Through Moral Authority

This one is for my late sister Robin "Oowey" McBride.

She was the heart behind so much of what we did, the reason Nay and I redirected that payment in the first place. She loved her three children fiercely and laughed every time she remembered that day: how AD thought he was getting paid, only to find out we'd handed the money straight to her. She understood it wasn't about shaming him—it was about standing up for her and those babies.

Oowey fought through cancer with a will that amazed us all. She wanted to live, not just for her children but for the grandchildren she did get to meet. She never lost the battle; she simply decided to lay down her gloves. Through it all she was proud of her brothers— her little big brothers—who grew into her protectors after she spent years protecting us.

I miss her every day. This book, like the barbershop, is another piece of armor and testimony for her. Rest easy, Oowey. Your "Big Bastard," as you always called me, is still holding it down—just like you always knew he would.

A-D had done the work. Wiring. Fixtures. Electrical hookups. No written contract—just a price agreed on: $450. A favor rate, really. We knew him. He had kids with my sister. Three of them. Beautiful babies.

But A-D had a habit. Not just the kind that comes in a bag, but the kind that makes a man disappear when he's needed most. He'd pop up broke, sleep on couches, eat up groceries—but when he got paid, he vanished.

He was never there for the birthdays, never there for the backpacks, never there with a bag of groceries. But he always showed up with two empty hands and a half-assed excuse.

So when the job was done at our shop, we drove to Queens. Not to see him. To see her. We handed the full payment to my sister. Our sister. Robin. Oowey.

We told A-D later, "Yo—we took care of it for you."

"You're kidding me, man," he said, blinking like we were joking.

We weren't.

"You don't have to worry about giving it to her," we said. "We did what you should've done—so you didn't have to drag yourself to do it."

He didn't bark. He didn't puff up. He knew. We gave him some gas money so he could make his way back. Because even men without shame still need a ride home.

And maybe we were out of pocket. Maybe it was a little strong-arm. But we didn't steal from him. We redirected the responsibility.

It was a garnishment. Not one handed down by the courts—but one handed up by us. A garnishment through moral authority. Through moral court.

Because she earned that money in pain. Because those kids deserved it. Because sometimes, Black men gotta step up for each other... at each other.

Because if you won't be a man for them, we'll be one in your place. And not with words. With money. Decisions. Actions.

And today, the boy named after A-D? He's ten times the man his father ever was. That's not shade. That's justice.

And every time I think about what we did that day—I don't flinch. I don't regret it.

We didn't rob him. We reminded him.

The Big Girl Theory

~In the Twinkle of Change

Some habits can change in the twinkle of an eye.

In the barbershop world, clients come and go. That's just part of the game. A customer might slide to another shop because it's closer to their job, because the hours line up better with their schedule, or even because the price fits their pocket. You never get salty about that. Habits change. People change. And a barber knows not to take it personal.

But when a client switches chairs inside the same shop? That hits different. That's when the dap gets a little weaker, the handshake gets a little shorter, and you start running back the tapes in your head — did I do something wrong? Did I slip?

That's exactly what happened the day Big Girl switched on me.

Now Big Girl wasn't a girl at all. He was a dude we nicknamed for his whole vibe — big, bald-headed, sweet-voiced, carried himself like your auntie's best friend who always had the gossip first. He'd been loyal to me for weeks, steady in my chair every two weeks on the dot.

I got him right, turned him from wolfing to sharp, and he let me know he appreciated it. Took selfies on his little flip phone. Tipped me good — ten-dollar cuts, twelve-dollar payments. A young client, but one I respected.

Then one Saturday, I walk in from grabbing food and he's sitting on the couch. I dap him up like always, "Yo, you ready?"

He looks right past me and points across the room. "I'm going to him." And just like that, Big Girl traded my chair for Nay's.

That's when I realized: you never stress when a customer walks out to another shop — you chalk it up to convenience or change. But when they stay in the building and just walk across the floor to another barber? That's when it stings.

The crazy part was, Big Girl had never even seen Nay cut. Didn't know his work. It wasn't about the haircut — it was about the crush. That's when the phone calls started, soft voice asking, "Is he there?" like Nay was the only man alive.

That's when the mirror stares started, Big Girl's eyes locked on Nay like he was watching the season finale of his favorite show.

And that's when me and Evel, the apprentice, set up the cookie prank — a plate of cookies wrapped in Saran Wrap, a note just sweet enough to make Nay nervous. When he walked in and saw that plate waiting on his station, he froze.

"Who left this here?" he asked, already side-eyeing the cookies like they were radioactive.

Evel, straight-faced as ever, said, "Yo, Big Girl dropped those off for you."

You should've seen Nay's face. Disgust, confusion, denial — all at once. And me? I had my back turned, pretending to clean my clippers, because if I looked at him I was cracking up. Of course, me and Evel broke open the cookies right there in front of him, talking about, "Yo, I don't know about you, but I'm hungry. No homo, I.m bouta smash these cookies!" while he sat there fuming, muttering about not knowing where those hands had been.

That was the moment he realized — whether he wanted to or not — Big Girl wasn't just a client anymore. He was a fan, maybe even a suitor. And it only got more real when Nay's girl — his now-wife — popped into the shop one day. The way Big Girl's vibe shifted? Like somebody blew out a candle. The twinkle turned to smoke. And just like that, the crush collapsed.

Funny thing is, once that dream shattered, he circled right back to me for cuts. Because no matter what, clients always return to the barber who first made them feel sharp.

Customers leave all the time, and you let them. But when they leave you for someone right beside you — especially someone they just caught a twinkle for — that's when you learn to laugh it off, hold your pride, and keep cutting. Because at the end of the day, most of them circle back anyway.

Big Girl sure did.

The Double V Campaign was a movement during World War II when Black Americans demanded two victories: one against fascism abroad, and one against racism at home. It started in the Pittsburgh Courier newspaper, but it lived in the hearts of every Black soldier who put on a uniform while still being denied basic rights in their own country. They fought on two fronts—one with weapons, the other with dignity and persistence.

For me, this history isn't distant. I had the honor of speaking regularly with a man who carried that fight himself. He wasn't just a veteran of war overseas, he was a veteran of the battle for respect right here at home. That's the legacy of the Double V—courage that demanded freedom in every direction.

I'm Sure He's Dead by Now

~A handshake with history echoing from the frontline

Every cut is a handshake with history — sometimes steady, sometimes trembling, but always sacred.

He shuffled in tall, sharp, and dignified — a man in his mid-to-late eighties who moved like time was scared to catch him. This was twenty years ago. By now he'd be well over a hundred. I'm sure he's gone. But back then, he was alive in every sense of the word.

He told me he'd fought in World War II, came home, and used his GI Bill to learn barbering. His brother was already a master barber. "I was the apprentice," he'd say proudly, and I'd grin at the way he said it every time, like I was hearing it for the first time. I never let him know I'd memorized his stories. I'd finish his sentences, not to correct him but to honor him, to make him feel seen. And when I nailed a line word-for-word, he'd beam, "Hot dog, you hit it on the nose!"

His stories were time capsules — Friday poker games in the back of the shop, him stationed in the front as the lookout. "They had more fun in the back than they did in the front," he'd whisper like it was a secret. "And prettier women too." Then he'd laugh so hard his whole body shook.

And I'd laugh with him, like we were two barbers swapping stories, not one man near the end of life and another at the start of his prime.

He'd take his hat off, run a wrinkled hand over his face. "You can't do much with this old mug," he'd joke, "but a barber makes you feel presentable — like somebody loves you. Makes you feel important." I've carried those words ever since.

Cutting his hair felt like shaking hands with history. My grandfather never came home from that same war. This man did. He walked back into a country that didn't respect him, didn't protect him, and he lived long enough to smile through it anyway — to sit in my chair and trust me with his dignity.

I don't know his name anymore. But I know his spirit. He's why I sharpen my lines with care. Why I still believe a barber's work is more than just a cut. It's restoration.

It's respect. It's a legacy passed hand to hand, clipper to clipper, from one generation to the next.

I'm sure he's dead by now. But he lives every time I make a man look in the mirror and smile. He reminded me that every time I pick up my clippers, I'm holding someone's dignity — and their history — in my hands.

I knew after his second visit that he wasn't just repeating himself; he was fighting the quiet erosion of memory. So, I let him tell it all again, word for word, like it was new — not to correct, but to honor. He was a soldier, a barber, a Black man who carried history on his back and still walked into my chair with dignity. To him, to my grandfather who never made it home, and to every soul who endured that war: your stories live each time I pick up my clippers. This work is for you.

When Politics Ate My Friend

Back in the Bronx our shop sat right in the middle of a civil-service hub: District 12 transit precinct on one side, a fire station on the other, the MTA offices across the street. We gave a $10 "civil service" haircut to cops, bus drivers, mechanics, dispatchers — a steady stream of men and women who kept the city moving. One of them was a white Irish-American bricklayer from the MTA. I won't use his name here. For years he was more than a client; he became a friend.

He'd bring his kids to the shop, I'd bring mine. We went to off-Broadway plays together. When a blizzard buried the Bronx, he stayed in the transit building and I slept in the shop, and later that night he drove his work truck through the snow so we could grab dinner at Frankie and Johnny's Pine. We talked about fatherhood, overtime, bad backs and good food. He was aware of the times, supportive when I told him about the cops choking me out, genuinely outraged at the injustice.

Even after I moved to North Carolina we kept the bond. I called him every August on his birthday. Once, driving his daughter to college in Florida, he jumped off I-95 just to stop at my house for a visit. We were from two different worlds but the respect was real.

Then something shifted. At first it was little rants on Facebook about halal carts "taking over" New York. Then he started liking comments from open racists in his feed — people using hard-R slurs about Black folks and Muslims. I called him out the Freezy way, joking but pointed: "Hey, this your boy?" He'd shrug it off — "Yeah, they're crazy" — but silence is compliance. Then came posts about South Africa, twisting uprisings against power into a "white-people-are-the-real-victims" story.

And then one day a video popped up in my feed with captions. January 6th. The Capitol. There he was. My friend from the shop, the man who once defended me, standing in a mob that had gone off the rails.

I still text him on his birthday. I'm not bitter. But it's wild to watch someone you knew as a decent, grounded father turn into a different person because politics stopped being an opinion and became a personality. Social media gave everyone a megaphone, and for some people it turned up the volume on their worst instincts.

When I look back I don't just see a friendship gone sideways; I see a cautionary tale. The barbershop taught me to listen to people without letting their storms drown me. It showed me how fast the world can spin somebody around. One day you're swapping snow-day stories over Italian food. The next you're watching them rage in a comment section and wondering how they got there.

That's the part nobody puts in the movies. In a real barbershop you see the whole arc of a man's life — the fresh cut, the slow fade, and sometimes, the sharp turn you never expected.

I remember when my sister Rose was 19 and voting in her first presidential election — George H.W. Bush versus Michael Dukakis. She took me with her to our elementary school, which was closed that day, and our mother was working the polls like always. Before we went into the booth I asked her who she was voting for. She looked at me and said, "None of your business." Then she added, 'That's why there's a curtain on the voting booth.

When Respect Costs a Client, So Be It

"Respect isn't optional — it's the entry fee to every interaction."—*Freezy the Barber*

It was one of those packed Saturdays in the shop. We prided ourselves on being organized — appointments, no marathon breaks, no twenty people waiting just to make the place look busy. But every now and then the shop would buzz like a beehive, chairs full, conversations bouncing, clippers singing. That day, my chair was turned just enough to catch the energy but not the source of it.

E was in my partner's chair. Caribbean brother, regular customer, brought his sons in, tipped well. Usually cool. But he had a habit of trying to be the wise guy, that brand of sarcasm that feels harmless to the one saying it but lands wrong on the one receiving it. Most of the time I let it roll. That day it didn't roll.

I'd had my back to him for a while, lining my own client, listening to the tone more than the words. He wasn't cursing or outright disrespecting, but you could feel the edge in his jokes, the way they were aimed at my partner instead of with him.

And something in me clicked. I spun around, clippers still in my hand, and said exactly what had been sitting in my chest: "Nah, bro. You're not doing that here. You come in here all the time doing that shit. Not today."

The shop went quiet like someone had hit pause on a movie. Even the music felt like it stopped. My partner looked up, surprised. He'd felt the disrespect but hadn't said anything. E looked stunned, like a father whose child just talked back for the first time. He tried to rebut, and I cut him off again, calm but firm.

I wasn't yelling, I wasn't threatening. I was drawing a line in my own space.

He finished the cut, paid, and never came back. My boy still jokes, "Yo, you cost me E's cuts — he paid good!" And maybe I did. But I'd do it again. Because that day I learned something every owner learns sooner or later: a shop's culture is worth more than a single customer. Respect has to be guarded as hard as the cash register.

I'm older now. I'd probably be more eloquent, maybe defuse it before it reached that point. But back then I was a young man protecting not just my partner but the vibe we'd built. The shop wasn't a clubhouse; it was a sanctuary. And sanctuaries have to be defended.

That moment stays with me because it showed another side of barbering. Sometimes the clippers in your hand aren't just tools — they're a line you hold steady. The same way I steady my wrist to protect a client's hairline, I had to steady my voice to protect my partner's dignity.

A clean fade grows back, but a clean culture lasts. In a barbershop, every boundary you draw with respect becomes part of the line you're teaching others to hold. Losing a client is temporary; losing your standards is permanent.

The Creditor Who Paid His Clients' Interest

I used to think giving a "family discount" was just what you do when you've got a skill. A cousin, a nephew, a neighbor brings their kid in for a cut, you hook them up, let them pay next week. You're the creditor now, right? But the math was upside down. Instead of earning interest, I was paying it.

Take my own sister. Before she ever gave me a chance, she stepped right over me and went to my boy Doobie who was older and more polished than young me to start cutting my nephew. I mean she got him an even all over caesar which was the easiest cut so I would've aced that task. She was a hover mom by nature, always standing over the barber's shoulder. Her excuse for sticking with Doobie was that my nephew was still developing his hairline and she didn't want to switch barbers once he started. Legitimate on the surface — but if she'd brought him to me first and not skipped over me, I could've been the one she stayed loyal to. Instead I wasn't prioritized, but they still expected me to prioritize them when money got tight.

Later, when I had my own shop, it was the same story at scale. Father, son, cousin in my chairs on a slow day — three heads, no money. I'd give "humble" cuts on credit while a paying client walked out the door.

My bread and butter, gone. I was the credit card company who lost money every swipe.

Eventually I learned. I didn't stop helping, but I stopped missing meals. If a paying customer came in while a "credit" cut was in my chair, I'd pause the favor and take the one who kept my lights on. Because if you had the money, you wouldn't be here asking; you'd be at Doobie's, or any other shop, paying full price without hesitation.

That's the hidden cost of credit in the barbershop. People who love you expect a deal; strangers respect your rate. And every time you extend that deal, you're the creditor who pays the interest — in lost time, lost income, and lost energy.

I'm still generous. I still cut kids for free when it matters. But I name the math now. Because respect for the craft is part of the cut. And if I don't respect my own time, no one else will.

The Night the Projects Roared, and Then Came the Noise

Once, the curtain on a voting booth signaled dignity and privacy — a quiet act rooted in struggle, sacrifice, and earned rights. In the glare of social media, that curtain has been ripped away, and politics has become a performance that can swallow whole friendships, families, even identities. In the barbershop you learn to listen without letting other people's storms drown you, to hold space for difference without surrendering respect. That discipline — to keep privacy sacred and humanity intact — may be the only way to keep the cut clean in an age when everything feels public.

The TVs in the barbershop glowed like scoreboards. The polls rolled in state by state, numbers climbing like batting averages, and the clippers hummed between conversations. My daughter sat in the corner, a broom in her hand, collecting quarters from cuss words like a bank teller on game night. Clients argued politics like Knicks vs. Lakers, voices bouncing off mirrors and Pergo wood floors. For once the debates weren't about street gossip or whose jumper was better. We were watching history form pixel by pixel.

She was nine, her smile too big for her face, her hope too heavy for her shoulders, but she carried it anyway. She had a poster in her backpack with Obama's name bold across it, pulled it out like a rally sign on the way home from school. She was campaigning harder than any adult I knew — not because she understood every policy, but because her teacher, Ms. Adams, a Ghanaian queen in heels and poise, told her she was royalty too. Representation does that. It lights a fire. It makes a child carry a man's dream like it's her own homework assignment.

We closed the shop, locked the gate, and walked home with that poster high. She waved it like a torch through Bronx streets lined with bodegas and tenements, past murals of Big Pun, past bus stops where hope was usually in short supply. The night smelled like fried food and Ocki Smoke Shop incense, but there was something else too: anticipation. The city buzzed low, like a current under our feet.

We ended up at my sister Rose's apartment, her window overlooking Park Avenue — the one in the Bronx — the Metro North tracks running like veins through the borough. We settled in, TV loud enough to drown out the trains, watching red and blue fill the map like rival gangs staking territory. My daughter tried to stay awake, her eyelids waging war with history, but she made me promise: "Wake me up when he wins." And I did.

When they finally announced it — when Barack Obama became the 44th President of the United States,

I shook her gently, and she sprang up like a firework. The apartment erupted in cheers, but the real noise came from outside. It started like a ripple — a few shouts, a horn or two — and then the projects roared.

The roar wasn't a cheer. It was an earthquake. A cathedral of sound from Butler Houses down Webster Avenue, from every balcony and window lit up like Christmas Eve. Cowbells clanged. Firecrackers popped. It felt like Yankee Stadium in October, bottom of the ninth, walk-off home run to win it all. Except this wasn't baseball. This was a borough, a city, a people, releasing 400 years of held breath.

I'd never seen joy like that in the Bronx. Never seen so many voices move as one — not for a parade, not for a championship. It was a choir of hope, an orchestra of disbelief turning into pride. For a night the streets weren't divided by tension. We were all neighbors, leaning out windows, ringing bells, screaming until our throats burned.

My daughter fell asleep again, but this time with a smile. She'd never know a world where a Black president was impossible. She'd grow up knowing that glass ceilings crack, that history bends, that the impossible is only temporary. Years later Journey would raise her tiny hand to mimic Kamala Harris, seeing herself in the first woman Vice President of the United States. My daughters will never know a time when they weren't reflected in the highest seats of power. And that's a gift worth writing down.

But me? I remember when that roar was unthinkable. I remember how long it took to echo. And I'll never forget the night the Bronx shook the sky because a Black man became President — an unintentional yet well-composed composition by an orchestra of hope.

But the roar didn't echo forever. Hope rang out that night, but in the years that followed it felt like someone turned down the celebration and cranked up the static.

Social media gave every whisper a megaphone, every keyboard a loaded weapon. We watched neighbors turn into strangers online, and strangers become bold enough to say out loud what they'd only muttered before. The world we dreamed of that night felt like it slipped through our fingers, replaced by comment section battles and headlines that bleed division.

The same Bronx streets that glowed that evening now buzz with a different energy. Fear and distrust linger in conversations that once brimmed with pride. And yet I hold on to that memory of my daughter's smile, her tiny fist clutching that campaign poster like a flag of promise. That night we believed history was bending toward us. And even if the noise came after — ugly, loud, and relentless — I still remember how loud hope was capable of being.

Every room becomes neutral ground when respect walks in first. — *Freezy the Barber*

Barbershop Diplomacy: Haircuts as Common Ground

You don't have to agree with someone to treat them with dignity.

Steel teeth buzzed like conversation starters, not weapons. Chairs turned into confessionals, a stage for neighborhood truths. Inside these four walls, badges and block reputations lost their edge.

The barbershop was neutral territory. The chair was Switzerland, the cape a peace treaty. On any given day, you'd see a cop in street clothes, a hustler with diamond chains, a bus driver talking overtime pay, and a single mom waiting for her son's cut—all in one room, one conversation, like puzzle pieces from different boxes that somehow fit.

We never had to announce who was who. No one needed introductions; the posture told you, the walk told you, the way they counted cash or carried keys told you. But the shop was a sanctuary. You weren't a badge, or a block legend, or a lawyer; you were just another man in the chair, arguing about whether LeBron would ever surpass Jordan.

Some cops wore their bulletproof vests under hoodies, their eyes scanning but soft, relieved to relax in a place where nobody flinched at their presence. Across from them, a dude fresh off the block, hands still smelling faintly of weed, talked to that same cop about joining the academy one day. That was the magic of the shop: the streets and the system could share air, share a laugh, share a respect they wouldn't get anywhere else.

And yeah, I've seen the other side. I've been choked by officers who saw me as a threat, seen friends thrown against walls, watched barbershops turn into crime scenes. But not here. Not my shop. We curated a space where integrity wasn't an option; it was policy. Men who hated cops and cops who hated being hated sat side by side and found something human in each other.

Haircuts were an excuse; the conversation was the real service. We set up job connections, introduced folks to the manager at Gristede's, helped kids fill out FAFSA, connected fathers to lawyers who understood custody battles. Taxes got done at the same counter where shape-ups were perfected. Our shop wasn't just where you got fresh—it's where you got direction.

In a city where tension simmered between blue uniforms and black hoodies, our little corner of the Bronx kept the spirit of the old-school barbershop alive: a safe haven, a roundtable, a cultural embassy. We were proof that a chair and a cape could be as powerful as any courtroom bench or pulpit.

And in that chair, whether you wore a badge or a bandana, you were just a man, trusting another man with a blade near your neck. There's something holy about that.

I don't know what it was about our shop but it always attracted young minds that wanted to learn, not just barbering but life. Even if it wasn't from us, there was always someone in the shop that the youth could learn from.

The Barber Pole

It stands outside like a lighthouse, spinning its colors into the street: red, white, blue — a spiral of history most people walk past without ever asking why. To most it's decoration. To us it's a banner. The oldest advertisement still turning in America.

Once upon a time a barber wasn't just a man with clippers. He was surgeon, dentist, healer. The pole came from that world. The red for blood, the white for bandages, the blue for veins. The ball at the top was the basin of leeches, the ball at the bottom the basin of water. The spiral motion echoed the towels barbers wrapped around patients' arms to make the veins rise before the cut. In Europe it was red and white. In the U.S., blue joined in — a sign of the veins, and maybe of the flag we stitched ourselves into.

Black barbers inherited that pole and gave it new meaning. In slavery days we weren't cutting our own people; we were cutting the planters and their sons. After emancipation the shop became the first Black-owned business many towns allowed — a place where a man could own his craft, his chair, his future. That pole outside meant: there is work, there is skill, there is a seat for you. Inside those walls we weren't just trimming hair; we were trimming trauma, stitching dignity, giving a man back his reflection the way a surgeon gives back a limb.

Every story you've just read lives under that pole. E's wise-guy sarcasm, the Mad Muslim hustling socks and bean-pie sermons, a boy nicknamed T-Rex sweeping floors for school money, Adam coming for blood on a chess board. All of it spinning together like the colors on that glass cylinder — humor, pain, hustle, redemption.

The pole is a memory and a promise. It tells a stranger walking by: you can come in from the storm. You can sit down.

Someone will touch your head with steady hands and send you back into the world a little cleaner, a little sharper, a little lighter. It's an unspoken oath to keep the space safe, to protect its culture the way the old-time barbers protected a patient's vein.
That's why, even in an era of LED signs and Instagram marketing, I still love the old pole. Because when it spins, it carries all of us — our history, our craft, our jokes, our scars — in one continuous ribbon. Red for the blood we've survived, white for the bandages we've wrapped around each other, blue for the veins that still run between us. A barber's life, a community's life, winding upward together, always in motion, always turning.

When I first learned what the barber pole actually meant, I was astonished. Mr. Hoover, who gave me my first chance in the barbershop at 14, was the one who explained it to me. All these years later I still feel the same sense of amazement, and whenever I share the story with others, they react just like I did. For a long time, like many people, I believed the pole simply represented the American flag swirling proudly outside the shop. Little did I know this profession stretches back long before America even existed.

In the barbershop you learn to add things up quietly and cut trouble off at the edge." – *Freezy the Barber*

On the Fence

He started choking me. Hands already behind my back, wrists offered without fight, I felt his arm snake around my neck, cutting off air that should have been mine. My first instinct was to raise a hand, to try and carve out an air passage, to protect myself. But I thought better of it. If I reached, if I struggled, they'd call it resistance. So I locked my arms still and tightened the muscles in my neck instead, absorbing the pain, refusing to give them the excuse they wanted.

It wasn't even the rookies who did it. The two in uniform, young and almost timid, had been speaking to me like a human being. They were respectful, careful, listening. Then came the sergeant — tall, bald, with authority in his voice but no badge on his chest — and with three words, "Cuff him up," my fate shifted. He never identified himself, but I assumed he was an officer. I gave up my wrists immediately. And then his arm closed around my throat. Later, when I asked him why, he told me he was afraid — because I was a big guy.

What they didn't see, what nobody asked about, was the truth. That morning I was simply trying to help my daughter's mother with a bill. Thirty-five dollars I had scraped together on a slow Tuesday, money I hadn't even eaten on. She wanted more, needed more, demanded more, and when I couldn't give it, she swung at me. She threw the first punch. All I did was restrain her, holding her hands so she wouldn't swing again. That's all it took for the world to tilt — for strangers to intervene, for her to weaponize the cops, for a sergeant who didn't know me to put his arm around my throat like I was a criminal.

The walkie-talkie came next. The same woman officer who had treated me respectfully at first cracked it across the back of my skull. She saw I was cooperating. She saw I had already offered my hands. She knew the sergeant was wrong — and yet she struck, leaving a gash that still sits there like a scarred memory. Then fists, elbows, boots, nine or ten cops piling on one man who had already submitted.

And then — salvation. It came by chance, and by seconds. At the transit station across the street, an announcement went out from the precinct — a woman being robbed. A false report. In the locker room, my boys were suiting up, about to start their shift underground, where they'd be out of sight, out of mind. If this had happened minutes later, they would have been gone. And I might have been injured, arrested falsely, carrying a record... or dead.

But they were still there. Dre, Lee, Travis, Austin. My boys in blue, but more importantly my brothers in life. They burst from the transit station, ready to jump into the fight until they realized the fight was me. Dre later told me, "I came running to get some elbows in — then I saw you, and I knew I had to stand on the other side." Travis shoved his own fellow officers back, planting himself in front of me, protecting me from the people wearing the same uniform he wore. Lee stood with him. Austin too. Dre pushed through, his voice cutting through the chaos.

In that instant, it wasn't about law, or protocol, or the thin blue line. It was about loyalty. It was about knowing who I was — a barber, a father, a man of that community.

And the community saw it too. They poured out of shops and apartments, following us down the street, cursing out the officers who had tried to break me. By the time I reached the precinct, it looked like a parade — people surrounding me as if I was their mayor, marching with me not in defeat but in defiance.

Inside, they removed the cuffs. The same sergeant who had choked me offered an apology, telling me about his own career nearly ruined by a woman's lies. I looked at him and wondered — if you know that pain, why did you give it to me? Why didn't you ask first? Why didn't you see me as you would see yourself? The answer, I knew, was simple. Because I wasn't him. Because I was a Black man in cuffs, and in his eyes, that was enough.

Dre is gone now. A heart attack took him on the basketball court he loved.

Lee was one of the first in New York to die from COVID. Travis is still here, carrying the weight of those losses. Austin too. I carry them all in this memory, because without them, I might not have walked away from that day.

So how do I feel about the police? I'm on the fence. Literally and figuratively. My body pressed against it as they tried to drag me down, my life saved by men in uniform standing on the same side of that line as me. I can't ever forget the chokehold, the blood, the humiliation. But I can't ever forget the protection either — the way loyalty and brotherhood rose up in the nick of time.

And maybe that's the truth nobody wants to admit. The system is rotten, the culture corrupt, but inside it, there are still men who will put their bodies on the line to shield you, even from their own.

I was beaten by cops. I was saved by cops. In the same encounter. And I'll never look at either side the same way again.

A Key With No Address, Open Sign, Closed Life

"Temporary struggle is proof you're walking toward a permanent vision." — *Freezy the Barber*

The gate rattled as I rolled it up from the night before, listening for footsteps on the sidewalk. Five-thirty in the morning—gray light creeping in, just enough to slip out unseen. To the world, I was early. To me, I'd never left.

I had a key, but no address. A barbershop to unlock, but nowhere to lock myself in at night. The shop couch was my bed, my coat my blanket, the sink my washroom. The same mirror I used to line up clients watched me scrub my face clean before sunrise, as if keeping my secret.

Nobody knew. Not even my partner. He thought I just got there early, never guessing I'd been guarding the shop in my sleep. My brother knew. Some nights, after the playoff games we hosted, he'd quietly pull the gate down for me—no judgment, no pity, just brotherhood. On the nights he wasn't there, I'd time the silence outside, wait for a gap between footsteps, and roll the gate down like magic. And at sunrise I was the guy who's always there early, sharp and ready to cut.

That was my reality—running a business without a home to go to. A barber with a key but no address, an "Open" sign glowing while my own life felt closed. I worked seven days a week for a period, nearly a thousand days straight, because if I didn't grind, the dream would die. And if the dream died, so would my chance to climb out.

Some days, I didn't eat. I'd sit in the empty shop, waiting for a six-dollar shape-up just to quiet the hunger pains that I never even felt in childhood. I made no doctor appointments, and took no time off— because a full day off in New York was too expensive when you're counting heads and not hours. So my health slipped, type 2 diabetes knocking on my door while I kept answering clients instead.

Yet, nobody could tell. Even then, people came to me for help, as if I was a man with everything in place. I carried myself like I had it, because image matters when you're cutting hair. No one wants a barber who looks broken.

So I smiled. I cracked jokes. I gave the sharpest fades I could, even when I hadn't eaten all day.

Looking back, I could've made better choices. Found another hustle, balanced things smarter. But the truth is, I'm proud of the dues I paid—not because it was glamorous, but because it was real. Those cold nights and empty stomachs taught me more about resilience than anything in this world. They showed me how far I'd go to protect a dream.

Now I stand here, a man who survived that struggle, who owns more than a key and more than a shop. But I'll never forget those mornings, that sound of the gate rattling as I pushed it up, the click of the lock, and the quiet pride of knowing I was building something when nobody else saw the blueprint.

I had a key with no address. And I turned it into a legacy.

A key with no address still means you're on your way home.

The Crevice, Reality that Swallowed Them Whole

Some places show you who people pretend to be; other places show you who they really are. Working in both worlds taught me that dignity isn't tied to the setting, it's carried by the person — and by the way you choose to treat them.

Friday and Saturday nights I'd step out of my shop and into a different world. The Wedge on Hunts Point — we called it "The Crevice" — felt like a 1970s blaxploitation set frozen in time: red lights, heavy bass, powder on mirrors. The women, some grandmothers now, still grinding because the game had never let them go. Girls paying tip-outs because they couldn't afford to tip in, taking cabs to swap their babies at their mothers' apartments just to come back and dance for nothing.

I wasn't there to party. I was there to work — a hundred dollars a night to bounce, search people at the door, keep my eyes open. And yet the images stuck to me. A man walks in with powder on his nose; I tap him, "You got a little something." He grins, "Just testing the product." Coke, cigarettes, shame, survival — all on display like some kind of dark theatre.

In the barbershop, I was the one holding clippers. In the club, I was the one holding a flashlight. Two different tools, same job: keep people safe, give them a moment of dignity.

Even there, in The Crevice, I tried to offer a little respect — a warning instead of embarrassment, a taxi instead of danger.

What it taught me was discipline. Eyes up, ears open. Never assume somebody's story by what you see at first glance. Some of those same men and women ended up in my chair later, clean-faced, talking like regulars. It also taught me humility:

I could be working all day in my own shop and still need to bounce at night just to stay afloat.

So when I opened the gate each morning, the smell of clippers and talc was my daylight after the underworld. And the lesson I carried back was simple: everybody's got a double life somewhere. What you see in front of you — whether it's a dancer, a hustler, or a barber — isn't the whole story.

Guardianship Cuts Both Ways

What my client is living through is not new; it's a modern echo of an old wound. Systems built centuries ago to tear Black men from their families still find quiet ways to repeat themselves today. Watching him fight to stay present in his daughter's life reminded me that the struggle to protect family is not just personal — it's historic, and it's ongoing.

It wasn't my life, but it mirrored pieces of it. A young Black soldier — one of my regulars — sat in my chair, rank on his sleeve, pain in his eyes. He'd just come back from six months in Somalia. Instead of a homecoming, he walked into a divorce and an all-out custody battle. His little girl adored him, but his wife — a white woman now using the system like a blade — had filed accusations, built a case, painted him dangerous. Overnight, this soldier turned from protector of a nation to defendant in family court.

I'd listen, cape around his shoulders, clippers in my hand, thinking about my own fight years earlier. How I wasn't biologically tied to my oldest daughter but fought like hell anyway. How I hid my own instability so she would never feel unstable. How a mother's anger can weaponize the courts, the cops, the whole world if you're not careful.

But his situation? It was relentless. He'd served on another continent only to come home to paperwork and supervised visits. I couldn't imagine the toll. Yet even as I cut, I admired his composure.

He didn't crash out. He showed up for his daughter in every way he could.

What that taught me — or maybe reminded me — is that fatherhood isn't just DNA or even daily presence. It's refusing to let someone erase you from a child's story, even when the system helps them try. Sitting across from him, I felt my younger self: broke, exhausted, but determined not to leave a child behind. Only now, at forty-four, I see it clearer: every father in my chair is fighting a war, some on foreign soil, some at home. And sometimes the barbershop is the only neutral ground where they can lay their armor down.

Someone asked me how I "get away" from barbering,
how I decompress from the grind and the weight of
other people's stories. Back then, the truth was upside-
down: my escape was the shop itself. The same four
walls where I was building a dream were also the
place where I hid from my own life. By day it gave me
purpose and connection; by night it held me in silence.
That's what "Trapped Inside My Escape" is about —
finding refuge in the very space that was also my cage

"Never give up your right to do right."

—*Freezy the Barber*

Trapped Inside My Escape

"What I thought was a setback was just the universe holding the door until I had all the right pieces"

—*Freezy the Barber*

From the outside, I was the man with the keys. The shop lights glowed, clippers hummed, laughter filled the room. People brought their worries and left with fresh fades, sharper edges, lighter hearts. They thought I went home at night to the same stability I gave them in my chair.

But the barbershop wasn't only a sanctuary for my clients. It was a sanctuary for me — a beautiful distraction. Holding other people's dignity in my hands meant I had to show my own. Nobody wants a barber who looks broken.

So I stayed clean. I kept my head up. I poured myself into their jokes, their confessions, their children's report cards. All day I cut hair, sharpened lines, mentored kids, smoothed over tensions. And then, when the last customer left and the lights clicked off, it was just me and that reality again.

I'd listen for the gaps between footsteps on the sidewalk, wait for the street to quiet, then pull the gate down from the inside.

In that moment the shop transformed. By day it was my stage. By night it was my cell. I was guarding it in my sleep, hiding in plain sight, waking up before dawn so nobody would know.

The same four walls that trapped me with my truth were also my escape from it. Daytime bustle and grind masked the night-time weight. Making people feel proud kept me from collapsing. Mentoring others helped me survive myself.

I'd almost forgotten all about that until it was just me — and that weight — alone behind the closed gate.

A Quiet Therapy Room

A barbershop can be both chair and confessional. Men walk in carrying weight, and even when you're carrying your own, you still become the steady hands and listening ears they expect. It isn't a mask of fakery; it's a discipline of strength — holding space so others can lay their burdens down, even if you have nowhere to lay yours. It's not fake, it's necessary.

I became a father before I was even a full-grown man. At barely eighteen I stepped into someone else's story and chose to be a father anyway. In the same way I stepped into barbering. No gap years, no warm-up. Straight from being a kid in the chair to being the one behind it — like Kobe and LeBron coming out of high school. By the time most barbers are still learning their craft, I was already an OG in "barber years."

That's part of why the shop has always been more than a hustle for me. It's been therapy. For them, for me. I'm licensed to cut hair, not to counsel, but somehow every clipper stroke becomes a confession. Men come in carrying their battles — overseas deployments, divorces, layoffs, fatherhood failures — and drop them on the floor along with the hair. They know I'm not going to use it against them. They know it stays in the shop.

And it goes both ways. When I was couching it in my own shop, hiding my exhaustion behind a clean lineup, it was the same ritual that kept me afloat: keep cutting, keep listening, keep showing up like I got it together.

You can't be hurting while you're making somebody else whole. That's the unspoken rule.

The old-school barbershop used to be a hub for everything. Taxes, notaries, hookups, advice, yellow pages before there were yellow pages. I've tried to hold on to that spirit — connecting clients with jobs, mentors, even just a word of encouragement from someone who's already been through what they're facing. I've watched strangers fix each other's do-rags, swap phone numbers, walk out a little sharper inside and out.

That's the part people don't always see. Behind the jokes and fades we're doing real work: protecting dignity, circulating information, catching a brother before he falls. We're not licensed therapists, but we're still therapists. We're pillows and blankets for a man's worries, but also the push that tells him to get up and do better.

I want that integrity back in every shop — rugged or polished, hood or suburban. Because if we do it right, a barbershop can still be what it always was meant to be: a sanctuary where boys learn to be men, men remember they're human, and everyone leaves with a little more hope than they brought in.

You Good Bro?

By Freezy the Barber

In the quiet moments, when the world doesn't see,

There's a weight we carry, heavy as can be.

We stand as the pillars, always holding strong,

Expected to be the heroes, never to go wrong.

But who asks the question, "You good, bro?" with care,

When the burdens get heavy and the load's hard to bear?

We're more than just providers, fixers of things,

We feel, we hurt, we dream, we worry about things.

In a world that demands we stay stoic and strong,

We swallow our pain, we've done it for so long.

But strength isn't silence, and tears aren't weak,

Sometimes we just need a safe space to speak.

To be seen as a human, not just a role,

To share in the journey, to lighten the toll.

So, brother, I'm asking, with all that I know,

From one heart to another, truly: You good, bro?

Invisible Collisions

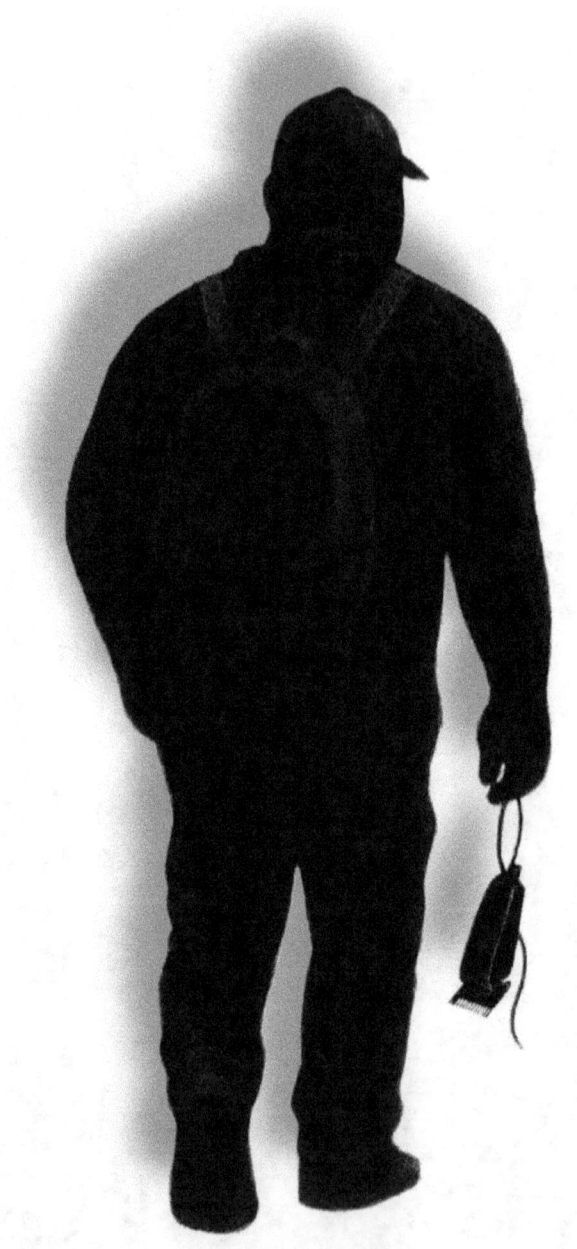

People always ask if my struggles ever bled into Dominae's life. The truth is, they did—just not where she could see them.

While I was sleeping on couches, in the back of a bar, sometimes in my car or behind my shop gate, she was at my mother's house or with her mom. I'd still show up every morning to take her to school, still pick her up every afternoon and bring her to the shop. She'd spend the day laughing, doing homework, sweeping hair for money, and collecting quarters for cuss words.

She never saw me pull the gate down from the inside and sleep behind it. She never knew about the police brutality incident her mother caused. All she knew was that her father had a shop, that it smelled like clippers and cologne, that it was full of stories and people who respected him.

That's the part of her life I wanted her to own. Whatever collided—money, housing, pride—it collided offstage. Onstage, all she saw was a dad who showed up.

"Manhood is not a destination. It is a quiet choice to show up when no one is watching. To break cycles without breaking yourself." —Freezy the Barber

How Do You Stop the Bleeding?

PAIN
STRUGGLE
STRESS ACCOUNTABILITY
DISCRIMINIATION
BELITTLEMENT
DISMISSIVENNESS
DEPRESSION
STRONG

When I was seventeen, already apprenticing but not yet licensed, I had to go down to the American Barber Institute in Manhattan to take the prerequisite exams. I wasn't a student there; I was learning in the shop. But to get my apprentice license I needed that certificate in "contagious diseases."

The instructor told me, "Answer one question and you can skip the test." He looked at me and asked, "How do you stop the bleeding?"

I didn't hesitate. "You apply talcum powder to the cut. It absorbs the blood and slows it down so you can dress it." He nodded and signed my certificate.

Back then it was a simple, practical answer — a barber's trick handed down through generations. Today the question hits different.

How do you stop the bleeding when it isn't on the skin but in a man's life? You can't stitch his wounds or fix the system that cut him.

But you can apply something: attention instead of powder, a listening ear instead of a bandage, a steady voice instead of gauze, a soft space where his pain can land without judgment.

In my chair a man can lay his pain down. I can't heal everything, but I can slow the hurt. I can give him a clean line, a moment of dignity, a safe place to breathe. Sometimes that moment is the only thing between him and giving up.

That's still barbering. We're still stopping the bleeding — just on a different layer now. From seventeen to forty-four, from talcum powder to quiet counsel, the work has changed and stayed the same. Hands steady, clippers steady, voice steady.

First you stop the bleeding. Then the healing can begin.

From Humbles to Homeowners,

There's a special kind of pride that comes from surviving the same storms with someone and still standing side by side years later. When the sacrifices finally turn into stability, the memories stop hurting and start shining — not because the struggle disappears, but because you both made it through. Sharing that journey with an old friend isn't just nostalgia; it's proof of how far you've come and how strong the bond became along the way.

Marcus wasn't the loudest or funniest guy in the shop. The magic was in our dialogue — the back-and-forth that turned two strangers into brothers. Twenty years later he's still my man. Back then, though, he was just a shy, humble dude trying to get his footing. His mother worked out at the Curves Gym next door. She and the other older ladies treated us like knights in shining armor, calling us whenever a "mouse" ran in. (It was really a Bronx chipmunk.) She told her sons about our shop; his brother Justin came first, then Marcus followed.

He walked in quiet, professional but hood, a few years older than me, already dealing with thinning hair and a receding line. He was thinking of shaving it bald — just giving up. I told him I could blend it, trim it down, keep a sharp line. At first he underestimated me. Clients who aren't barbers can't see what a barber can see. Finally, he gave me a chance and I kept him looking good for years. He's bald now, but that cut held him down for a long time.

Our friendship started with a movie quote.

While he hesitated over the haircut, I cracked a line from Juice: "This n***a's scared." Without missing a beat he shot back, "I ain't scared, Bishop. I just told you I got a DJ Saturday night." Total strangers, perfect timing. From that day on we've been quoting movies, sharing our love for classic rock music and clowning each other like brothers. The yo-mama jokes we trade would make outsiders think we're enemies. In reality, we were two good guys dealt bad hands — chasing dreams, pushing through sacrifice, trying to be fathers and make ends meet.

Sometimes he needed a "humble" — a haircut on credit. Sometimes I needed an $80 loan. We looked out for each other. Now we're both at the peak of our games, happily married, families thriving, homes and careers secure. Every time we talk we laugh about those days and how far we've come. From humbles to homeowners. From a scared client to a lifelong friend.

Old School in a New Room

People who walk into my shop for the first time are usually surprised. They expect noise, multiple chairs, TV blaring, clippers buzzing from every corner. Instead, they step into a single-room studio built onto the side of my house. One chair. One mirror. Black history on the walls—Negro League baseball photos, Miles and Coltrane album covers, shelves of books by Black authors I admire.

Jazz, old soul or classic hip-hop humming low in the background. Everything in that space is a conversation piece, a memory waiting to be triggered.

It's not the size of the shop that makes it feel alive; it's the spirit inside. I've created what a lot of people call "the old-school barbershop" even though the barbershop culture outside my door has thinned out. Guys who grew up sitting all Saturday in the shop, soaking up gems from grown men, now tell me they can't find that anywhere else. But when they come here, they feel it again.

Oz said it best just a few days ago. He's twenty-seven, a sharp young brother with his head on straight.

He and another client—same age, equally solid—started talking politics and life while I was lining them up. Mid-conversation Oz leaned back, looked around, and said, "Man, this is what I remember. This is what we used to do. Sit in the shop, listen, learn." For a minute it was like we were in a Bronx barbershop circa 1999 instead of a one-chair room in Fayetteville.

That moment confirmed for me why I've kept this atmosphere alive. I don't have a crew of barbers anymore. I don't have a waiting area full of people playing dominoes. But I have a steady stream of conversations that matter. We argue sometimes. We agree sometimes. But we keep it constructive. People leave a little sharper in the mind as well as the hairline.

I call it a boom-boom shop because it's small but powerful—like a speaker that hits hard even at low volume. This is where young cats see what respect looks like, where they can ask a grown man about money, marriage, faith, or politics without getting clowned. It's where a father can bring his son and both of them can relax their shoulders.

It's where stories pass from one generation to the next without a syllabus or a test.

That's the invisible curriculum at work again. You can't teach it in school. You have to live it. A boy watching how I greet an elder. A young man watching how I defuse tension. A father listening while his son gets advice on college. It's subtle, but it sticks.

Years from now they'll remember the smell of talc and aftershave and the sound of a lesson landing.

And don't get it twisted—this one chair isn't a step down; it's a deliberate choice. I built my legacy already. I'm the GOAT on the app I use, booked steady for years, mentoring other barbers even from this small shop. I don't need a storefront with neon to prove my worth or pull in walk-ins; clients seek me out. Soldiers rotate through Fayetteville and leave for Germany or Hawaii or civilian life and still keep in touch because the bond went beyond the cut. I'm not trying to beat anybody over the head with prices.

I'd rather build a steady flow of people who want to be here, who know they're getting the best haircut of their life and a conversation they can trust.

Even from the privacy of my own shop, I'm still in the community—free back-to-school cuts, church events, mentoring programs. Some people I help have never sat in my chair. That's fine. The impact isn't smaller just because the space is smaller. In some ways it's bigger, because it's concentrated.

This is why Faded into Truth exists. It's the book version of this room: a place where you can hear the stories behind the cut, the lessons between the lines, the gems dropped without fanfare. The shop is my pulpit, my classroom, my confessional and even if it's just me and one client at a time, the legacy is collective.

Legacy in the Mirror

When I glance up at the mirror mid-cut, angling a client's head for the next pass of the clippers, I still see the same eyes I saw at seventeen. Back then I was in awe that I was even standing behind the chair. Cutting hair was the position I'd dreamed of since I was a kid, and every time I caught my reflection it was like proof I'd made it. Even now, decades later, I still steal those glances.

The man looking back at me has gone through stages — chin-strap beards, the awkward pre-pubescent moustache paired with a grown-man jawline, the scars and the breaks. I can literally see my story mapped on my face. The scar from brain surgery sits above my temple like a reminder: there was a mass growing in my head all those years I was building my craft, and I didn't even know it. The mass is gone now, but the scar remains, a visible proof that I survived. My smile is fuller, my teeth better. My body is bigger, huskier, but my presence is steadier.

What strikes me most is the difference in my eyes. At seventeen, they were eager, ready to take on any challenge a head of hair could throw at me. Now they're confident. It's not just that I'm willing to face a challenge — it's that I know I can. I can turn any client into the best version of himself. There's a quiet comfort that comes from mastery. My forehead doesn't sweat the way it used to; my hands move with calm assurance.

Even my beard has become a signature — black on the sides with a perfect natural gray streak down the middle like a skunk tail, the kind of detail people assume I dyed on purpose. That stripe has become its own calling card, the mark of a man who's grown into his craft.

Sometimes I wish I'd had this knowledge back then. But if I had, maybe I wouldn't have grown into the man I am now. I might have thought I knew it all already.

There's truth in that old line about youth being wasted on the young, but in my case my youth wasn't wasted; it was invested. Those years of learning, sweating, failing, and trying again were how I built myself.

What I see now in the mirror isn't just a barber. It's a student-teacher. Even as a griot, even as the OG in the room, I'm still learning. I pick the brains of the young cats who sit in my chair. I let them explain their world so they feel their own ethos. I take what they know about technology or hustle or culture and weave it back into my own lessons about craft, discipline, and manhood.

That's why the first piece in this book had to be about "The Chair Is Sacred." Even though the book was already forming in my mind, that conversation convicted me to start it there. It reminded me that I'm still a student of the game. Still learning in order to teach.

So when I catch my reflection now at the end of the day, I see all of it — the kid in awe, the man with scars, the griot still taking notes. I see the hairlines I've saved and the lives I've witnessed. Barbering didn't just reshape hairlines; it reshaped me. And every time I look in that mirror, I see a better version of the same man who first picked up the clippers and thought, "This is it."

Sawdust

The smell of sawdust still turns my stomach. Hot, sharp, and clinging to the back of my throat, it was the perfume of trial and error — of ambition in work boots. We didn't know a thing about building, but we knew how to create. So we cut Pergo boards on the floor of 1184 East 180th Street, hands raw, lungs coated in dust, laying down underlayment like a prayer mat. Every plank we set was a promise: this shop would be ours.

Aggrey strung wires through drywall, anchored TVs from the ceiling like ornaments of success. We rolled paint on every wall ourselves, sweat dripping into every stroke. And somehow, in that small Bronx storefront, we birthed a space that felt like a downtown loft dropped in the hood. It smelled of hustle, looked like respect. Nobody had to be told how to act when they walked in — we didn't demand it. We commanded it.

I hated sawdust then, still do now. But even as the scent makes me grimace, it carries pride. It reminds me of who I was becoming: a business owner, a barber who had carved out more than just haircuts — a future. We weren't just barbers; we were architects of integrity. Every screw, every brushstroke, every aching back and calloused hand was a declaration that this craft was sacred. That shop taught me to respect the business even more. That shop made me a griot. That shop made me a man.

Sawdust is still my least favorite smell. But it's also the sweetest memory I know.

Transcendent Lessons

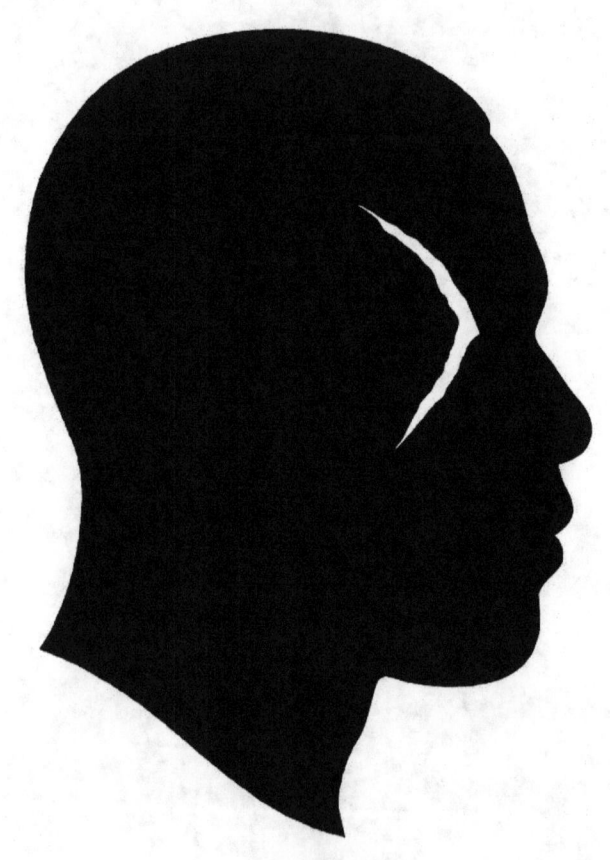

Nobody taught me this in a classroom.

It didn't come from barber school or a licensing manual.

It came from the chair, from the stoop, from the men who sat down and told the truth without knowing they were teaching me.

One of the first lessons was etiquette — not the fork-and-knife kind, but the street kind. How to read a room, how to respect another man's space without shrinking your own.

I remember a client almost twenty years ago. Fresh out of jail, a scar running down his face like a lightning bolt. He looked grimy, dangerous even. But as soon as he sat down, I could see the other side of him: polite, articulate, happy to be free. He told stories, asked questions, listened. That scar made people assume he was the storm; but really, he was the one who'd been struck.

My boy Rick crossed paths with him a lot back then. Rick's one of the nicest dudes you'll ever meet, but he walks and dresses like he's ready for a fight. He swore the scarred guy was mean-mugging him, looking for beef. For years he held onto that idea. And for years I kept telling him, "He's not like that. You're both reading covers, not books."

Two decades later Rick finally understood what I meant.
Sometimes a look isn't a threat; it's just curiosity, or habit, or the residue of survival. Sometimes the toughest face belongs to the gentlest man. Sometimes the guy staring at you is only trying to figure out if you're safe.

That's the invisible curriculum of the barbershop.
You learn patience without anyone calling it a virtue.
You learn to read people without judging them.
You learn that every scar has a story, and most of the time the person wearing it didn't give it to himself.

You learn that your own appearance tells a story too, and it might not be the one you think.

Those lessons shaped me more than any clipper technique. They made me a better barber, a better businessman, a better man. Because if you can see through a person's armor, you won't block your own blessings. You won't miss out on a connection, a client, a friend, a future.

Now I pass that on to the younger cats in my chair. I tell them:
Don't just look at the scar.
Ask yourself who gave it.
Don't just read the cover.
Let the book open.

That's the curriculum nobody writes down but everybody can learn — if they sit still long enough, like in a barbershop, and watch.

Sometimes a lesson takes years to land. Back then Rick swore the man with the scar was trouble; I kept telling him he wasn't. Two decades later he came back and said, "You were right." That's not about ego. That's about growth. It takes strength to admit you misread someone, to see past the cover to the book. The barbershop teaches that without ever calling it a class: patience, humility, and the courage to say, "I was wrong."

"No" Is a Complete Sentence

"Demanding respect is telling people how to treat you; commanding respect is showing them. Set the tone with who you are, and you'll never have to ask for it."
— *Freezy the Barber*

He came into the shop with the same look I've seen a hundred times: fresh out of prison, fresh out of luck, and trying hard to look like neither. He was the older brother of one of my mentees—a kid who hung around the shop dreaming about rap because he didn't have many examples of men standing still and building something.

His brother was older than me by a year or two, claiming Blood, wearing the hard shell that comes with it. Chains, bravado, stories about Far Rockaway and about "getting over" on his parole officer. Maybe some of those stories were true; maybe they were tall tales. Either way, I could see through him. Under the shell he was more foolish than fierce.

At first I gave him grace. When a man is trying to re-enter society, the least I can do is keep him looking presentable. He was broke, looking for work, at least saying he was.

So I gave him a "credit cut" a few times, hoping it would help him land something and start paying for his own upkeep. But he kept coming—week after week—without calling, without paying, and without showing any sign of change.

And the energy he brought in with his crew was starting to contaminate the space. Loud. Posturing smelling like dirt weed. The kind of energy that makes other clients uncomfortable. I had to check them—this is my shop, not a clubhouse—and tell him not to bring his homies back to my shop.

By the third "credit cut" I realized what was happening: I wasn't helping him stay presentable for a job; I was helping him stay fresh for whatever else he was doing. And I was losing money and risking my atmosphere in the process.

That's when I drew a line.

When he sat down again, I looked him in the eye and said, "You're trying to be fresh, bro, but you can't afford to be fresh. I'm not cutting you for free anymore."

He stared at me, confused. So I asked him a question I knew would give me the answer I needed:

"Are you gay?"

He blinked. "No."

Exactly. No. One word. A complete sentence.

I told him, "That's how I'm answering you. I'm not explaining. I'm not saying 'I can't' or 'I don't have time.' I'm saying 'no.' Period. That's it."

He tried to reason with me, but I didn't budge. He left, and that was the last time I saw him. I didn't care about the money. I cared about the principle.

Because here's the invisible curriculum in that moment: compassion is not the same as being a doormat. When you run a shop, when you run your own life, you have to know where your help ends and their responsibility begins. Otherwise you become an enabler, not a mentor.

"No" is a complete sentence. It's a boundary. It's self-respect. It's also a way of teaching someone else what respect looks like. And in a neighborhood where favors, family discounts, and street politics can twist a man's business into knots, learning to say "no" without apology might be the most valuable skill of all.

The Invisible Curriculum

(the full lesson)

Nobody ever wrote this into a textbook.
It's not on a state board exam or in a business plan.
It's the syllabus you only get by living it — by
sweeping floors, cutting fades, listening, watching.
It's the invisible curriculum of the barbershop, and it's
been shaping me since I was a teenager with clippers
in my hands.

Lesson One: Etiquette You Can't Google

One of the first lessons was etiquette — not the fork-
and-knife kind, but the street kind. How to read a
room, how to respect another man's space without
shrinking your own. How to make somebody feel safe
without making yourself small.

I remember a client almost twenty years ago. Fresh out
of jail, a scar running down his face like a lightning
bolt. He looked grimy, dangerous even. But as soon as
he sat down, I could see the other side of him: polite,
articulate, happy to be free. He told stories, asked
questions, listened.

That scar made people assume he was the storm; but really, he was the one who'd been struck.

My boy Rick crossed paths with him a lot back then. Rick's one of the nicest dudes you'll ever meet, but he walks and dresses like he's ready for a fight. He swore the scarred guy was mean-mugging him, looking for beef. For years he held onto that idea. And for years I kept telling him, "He's not like that. You're both reading covers, not books."

Two decades later Rick finally understood what I meant.
Sometimes a look isn't a threat; it's just curiosity, or habit, or the residue of survival. Sometimes the toughest face belongs to the gentlest man. Sometimes the guy staring at you is only trying to figure out if you're safe.

Lesson Two: Scars and Stories

That's the invisible curriculum of the barbershop.

You learn patience without anyone calling it a virtue.

You learn to read people without judging them.

You learn that every scar has a story, and most of the time the person wearing it didn't give it to himself.

You learn that your own appearance tells a story too, and it might not be the one you think.

I've cut the hair of cops and ex-cons, teachers and hustlers, fathers and sons. Sometimes they're all in the same room at once. Sometimes a man who's just come home from doing ten years is sitting two chairs away from a rookie officer getting his first fade. In those moments, my shop isn't just a shop; it's neutral ground. It's a classroom where everyone's both student and teacher, whether they realize it or not.

Lesson Three: The Mirror Works Both Ways

The mirror in front of the chair isn't only for the client. It's for me.

Over the years I've caught my own eyes in that glass — at seventeen, at twenty-five, at forty-four — and watched myself grow. My forehead doesn't sweat like it used to because I'm comfortable now. My hands move with confidence. My beard has become my signature: black on the sides with a perfect gray streak in the center, like a badge I didn't have to buy.

When I was younger, every cut felt like a test. Now it feels like a conversation. And the biggest difference isn't technique; it's patience. Back then I rushed to prove I belonged. Now I know I belong. That's another piece of the invisible curriculum: learning to see your own evolution while you're still in motion.

Lesson Four: Opening the Book

I tell the younger cats in my chair: Don't just look at the scar. Ask yourself who gave it. Don't just read the cover. Let the book open. Some of the best connections you'll ever make are with people who look nothing like what you expected.

220

If you close that door too soon, you might block your own blessing.

I've had clients who started as strangers and ended up guiding me through business decisions, connecting me to opportunities, even praying for me when my mother passed. None of that would've happened if I'd judged them by the first impression.

Lesson Five: Passing It On

Now, in my own shop built onto the side of my home, the walls lined with Black history photos and shelves of books, I try to recreate what I got as a kid — the old barbershop vibe where you could learn a thing or two just by sitting still. My younger clients, like Oz and his friends, come in and talk politics, business, fatherhood. They stay after their cuts just to listen, the way I used to.

That's when I know the invisible curriculum is still alive.

It didn't die with the old heads or the corner shops. It's in every conversation, every warning, every gem dropped between clippers buzzing. It's in the way a man with a scar can find respect instead of suspicion, and a man with a tough walk can find understanding instead of fear.

Closing the Lesson

Those lessons shaped me more than any clipper technique. They made me a better barber, a better businessman, a better man. Because if you can see through a person's armor, you won't block your own blessings. You won't miss out on a connection, a client, a friend, a future.

That's the curriculum nobody writes down but everybody can learn — if they sit still long enough, like in a barbershop, and watch.

That's My Mirror

Sometimes you're only seeing a work in progress, not the finished picture. The one shaping it needs space to step back, study, and adjust. In every craft, relationship, or dream, the unseen stage belongs to the maker. Trust the process long enough for the reveal to show you what patience created.

Every chair has two mirrors: the big one at the station and the little one at the end. The big mirror is mine. It's how I see the cut as it's forming, the way a painter steps back from a canvas. The small mirror I hand you at the end—that's yours. That's the reveal.

Sometimes my body language confuses people. When I take a few steps back, clippers in my hand, tilting my head to the side, it looks like I'm presenting your hair to you—like I'm silently saying, "Look." But I'm not. I'm looking. I'm checking my work from a distance so I can see what the close-up view hides. It's my way of measuring balance, symmetry, and flow before I move on.

The big mirror isn't about vanity or ego; it's my gauge. With that glass and light I can see details no naked eye can catch—the stray hair breaking the silhouette, the taper that needs another pass, the neckline that wants a tighter angle. When you're swiveling to peek mid-cut, you're looking at an unfinished sketch. You can't see what I'm shaping, and you're blocking my view.

I tell clients all the time: trust the process. Respect the craft. In your world—whether it's logistics, medicine, electrical—I'd be lost. That's why you do what you do and I do what I do. The big mirror lets me give you my best work. The little mirror at the end lets you see it.

Business Versus Calling

People think barbering is about clippers and cash. They see the shop, the steady flow of heads, the phone buzzing, and they assume it's a small business like any other. But for me it's always been more than a hustle. It's been a calling.

When I started, I didn't even have enough to cover my own chair rent some weeks. What I did have was a chair, a pair of hands, and the example of barbers before me who doubled as counselors, historians, and guardians. Even now, decades later, when the shop is on my own property and the walls are lined with Black baseball photos, jazz records, and books from writers I respect, the heartbeat is the same.

I give haircuts, yes. But more than that, I build trust. People sit down in my chair not only because they like my fades, but because they know they can exhale. They bring their pain, their secrets, their hopes. They know I'm not going to swat them down or clown them. If anything, I'll boost them up.

Even guys who don't trust anyone else will open up to me. That isn't a business transaction. That's stewardship.

Over the years I've learned the difference between a job and a calling. A job asks, How much will I get paid for this hour? A calling asks, What will I leave behind after this hour? When you see it that way, you still have to charge fairly, but money stops being the main scorecard. My goal has never been to capitalize on my community but to help sustain it—whether that's a clean cut before a job interview, a word of encouragement before a court date, or just letting somebody sit and breathe in peace for a few minutes.

That's also why boundaries matter. Early on I thought being generous meant saying yes to every "put it on my tab" request. Family, friends, guys out of prison trying to get on their feet—I'd float them cuts, loan a few dollars, keep them looking presentable. Sometimes it helped. Sometimes it just kept them fresh for the club while my own rent was late.

I had to learn that no is also an act of service.
No protects my craft, my livelihood, and the dignity of the person in my chair.

There's an old-school ethic I try to keep alive: give people a glimpse of goodness right in their own neighborhood. Let them see that good people still exist. Let them experience professionalism and respect without having to go downtown or sign a contract. That's why the books matter too. Painting With Words and Faded Into Truth aren't side hustles to squeeze more dollars out of a haircut—they're my way of putting the same trust, the same stories, into print so they can travel beyond my four walls.

I've never believed that money can buy respect. In fact, some of the most disrespectful moments of my career happened when somebody thought their cash entitled them to treat me any kind of way. Respect comes from consistency, from keeping your word, from showing up with skill and heart over time.

The men and women who sit in my chair know I'm there for them.

That's what keeps them coming back more than any price list ever could.

Business pays the bills. Calling feeds the soul. I've learned to balance both: steady hands, steady books, steady voice. But at the end of the day, the legacy I'm building isn't just a roster of clients—it's a neighborhood of people who've seen that goodness up close, who've felt dignity restored one cut at a time.

Suddenly the OG

Yo I don't know how it happened but one day I was a kid, then I looked up and young dudes began calling me Unk an OG. I didn't plan it, it just happened. And I'm good with it — I take it as a sign of respect. I've earned my stripes, and it feels right to embrace it."

I still catch myself thinking of "old heads" as somebody else — men with salt in their beards, a certain weight in their voice, stories from decades I wasn't even born in. In my mind they were the ones teaching, warning, laughing at our mistakes while handing us game for free. I never pictured myself as that man. Yet here I am, mid-forties, beard streaked with gray, young brothers calling me "Unk" without irony.

It snuck up on me the same way a perfect fade takes shape: slow, steady, almost invisible until you step back and look at the line. One day I realized the soldiers in my chair were nearly twenty years younger than me. They were going through their first divorce before twenty-five, their first deployment, their first real heartbreak. They're trying to hold it together, trying to look the part. And they sit in my chair because they trust me not just with their hair but with their thoughts.

I see my younger self in them. The ambition. The mistakes. The hunger to be seen and to matter. I remember when I was looking ahead to the years I'm living now — never sure I'd even reach them. Back then I thought OGs were born that way. I didn't know you earned it cut by cut, decision by decision, standing your ground when it counted, learning when to be quiet, when to give someone a chance, when to say no.

Being the OG isn't about a title; it's about stewardship. It's about telling a young client, "Nah, you can't keep running up credit cuts" because he needs to hear "no" from a man who still respects him. It's about giving a soldier a book off my shelf or a story from my own scars so he knows he isn't alone. It's about holding the line of excellence so that a haircut becomes more than a haircut — it's a standard for how you show up in the world.

I don't need a big shop or a flashy platform to validate that. My impact stretches far beyond this one-chair room. Guys who were once stationed at Fort Bragg still send me messages from Germany, Kuwait, civilian life. They show me pictures of their weddings, their businesses, their kids. They still call me "Freezy" or "OG." That's legacy.

I never imagined myself as an elder. But the truth is I've been preparing for it since I first picked up clippers. Every story I listened to, every mistake I owned, every lesson I passed on without charging for it was practice for this role. And now that I'm here, I wear it with humility and pride.

Because being the OG isn't just about having years behind you. It's about staying curious enough to keep learning, generous enough to keep teaching, and steady enough to be trusted. It's about standing in that barbershop mirror at the end of the day, seeing the same eyes you had at seventeen, and knowing they've grown wise without growing cold.

When the Sponge Becomes the Well

I was once the quiet kid in the corner,
ears open, hands steady, eyes wide—
a sponge in a sea of clippers and talk,
soaking up more than fades and tapers,
catching wisdom as it dripped from old hands
and watching fathers build kingdoms on a lunch break.

Years passed like hair on the floor.
Every sweep of the broom, every story told
sank into me until I was heavy with lessons—
how to work with care,
how to hold a child's trust,
how to stand tall when life sits you down.

Now the sponge is full.
It's my turn to wring out what I've gathered—
knowledge, patience, manhood, fatherhood—
pouring it into new hands, new hearts,
so they can soak up what was once poured into me.

I never noticed the shift
until the young ones started calling me "OG."
But that's the cycle—
to learn, to live, to teach,
to pass the water forward
without losing the well inside yourself.

Behind the Chair but Ahead of the Game

I've never been able to keep my work inside four walls. Even when I'm standing behind the chair, I'm already looking beyond it. The clippers in my hand might shape a fade, but my mind is shaping something bigger — a book, a show, a way of turning one small act into a ripple.

That's how I've always moved. When I cut hair, I don't just cut; I build trust, I mentor, I stage conversations. When I write, it's not just another book; it's a whole imprint, a movement. When I try a hobby, I find a way to fold it back into the bigger story. Poetry, stand-up comedy, singing in a rock band — they all feed the same pulse. My shop becomes my stage. My chair becomes a microphone.

I don't know where I learned to stretch everything past its first purpose. Maybe it's because, growing up, nothing we did was ever "just for fun." Every hustle had to serve a bigger need. Or maybe it's because I've always been a student of possibility. Whatever I pick up, I look for the bigger picture hiding inside it.

I elongate it. I expand it. I refuse to let it be one-and-done.

That mindset is why I wasn't content to just cut hair. A lot of barbers work their whole lives without ever owning a shop. Within ten years of picking up clippers — and only about four or five years after I was old enough to even be an apprentice — I opened my first barbershop at twenty-four. I didn't do it to show off; I did it because I could already see the future I wanted to build. Me and Nay always had our minds outside the norm. Everything was a steppingstone for us.

That's what "ahead of the game" means to me. Not about being flashy or beating someone else, but about seeing angles others don't, and then giving those angles away — to clients, to readers, to the next young person who steps into my shop thinking it's only about a haircut.

We used to stand behind the chair, but our eyes were always on something bigger. Back when we were just kids cutting hair side by side, we were already sketching blueprints in our heads — schools, mobile services, new ways to reach people. We opened a barbershop together when I was only 24 and he was 28. Today Nay runs Westchester Barber Academy, and I run Mobilstyles Hair Grooming Services, bringing hair care to adults with developmental disabilities. We've both built the visions we used to discuss between cuts. Behind the chair but ahead of the game — that was always us. Salute to my brother Nay.

"What seems flawless to the eye is often a quiet dance of adjustments you'll never notice. True craft bends reality until balance feels like truth."

—*Freezy the Barber*

Optical Illusions

~Straight Lines on a Round Head

People think a perfect line-up is just a matter of drawing a straight line. They don't realize they're asking for the impossible: a straight line on a round head. Every sharp edge you've ever admired in a barbershop is an optical illusion.

A barber reads the head the way an architect reads a blueprint—scanning curves, bumps, growth patterns. I might extend one temple point a fraction, or lower the other, so that the line across your forehead appears level. Sometimes the top line has to tilt a hair's width for your hairline to look even. That's the craft.

Clients rarely see the adjustments, they just see the result and call it "perfect." But "perfect" is really "balanced," not "straight." It's the art of making the eye believe. That's why, when someone cranes their neck every time I lift my clippers, it slows the process. The mirror at my station is my instrument, not theirs. In that mirror, with the light falling just right, I can see stray hairs and asymmetries the naked eye misses. It's the only way to sculpt precision on a living canvas. Life's a lot like that, too. Sometimes you have to shape things slightly off-center to make them appear true. It isn't deception; it's care and craftsmanship. Most of the straight lines you admire are really curves guided with intention.

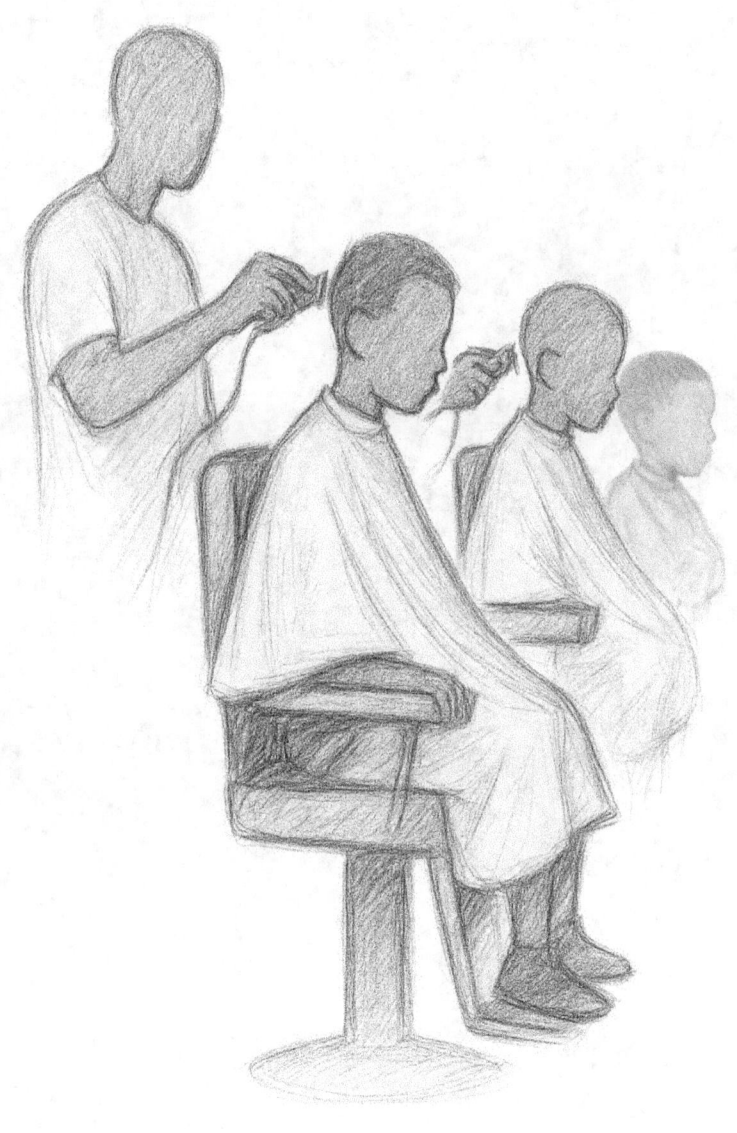

The Big Alma Special

I can still hear my mother's voice at the shop door: "Tell him that's all I've got — take it or leave it." Three boys, twenty dollars, seven-dollar cuts. It wasn't haggling; it was survival. She wasn't trying to cheat anyone. She was doing the math of a woman raising a houseful of kids on welfare and food stamps. My I don't recall my father ever paying for our haircuts. My mother made sure we still got them. She fed extra mouths, took in nieces, nephews, friend's kids, and somehow still scraped up to keep her boys up. When I think of strength and advocacy, I don't picture speeches; I picture her handing us that twenty and saying, "Go get your hair cut." That was her way of holding us down.

One of the reasons I became a barber traces back to those Saturday trips to Cameo's Barbershop on Third Avenue. Before it was Cameo's it had been Heavy's, tucked between the Spanish church and Holy Tabernacle. It was a small shop connected to a tenement building that never seemed to have tenants, but to me it was the whole world. That's where I first smelled clipper oil and talc, where I first sat on cracked vinyl and watched men become sharper versions of themselves.

My mother sent us there when she could. We didn't have much, but when she scraped together a haircut fund she'd press a twenty-dollar bill into our hands and send three boys off to the shop. Haircuts were seven dollars each. We were always a dollar short, no tip, no cushion — just my mother's voice telling us, "That's all I got. Tell him take it or leave it." Cameo would sigh but he cut us anyway. He was young himself back then, a light-skinned brother in his twenties running his own shop, with Darren and Derrick on the other chairs.

They were the first barbers I ever studied.

Those Saturdays planted two seeds. One was grace. I know what it's like to be the family that's a dollar short, so I've always had patience for clients who are genuinely trying but just don't have it. The other was a kind of hunger. I don't recall my father ever paying for my haircuts. My mother was the one advocating, stretching, making sure we were presentable. She bought house clippers too, but her DIY cuts were disasters — part Baldy, part Caesar, no line-up. I remember hiding at the back of the lunch line so nobody would see the back of my head, dodging the saliva slap kids gave when somebody had a "Baldy bean."

Somewhere between those crooked home cuts and those six dollar and thirty three cents shop cuts, I decided I wanted to learn. I didn't just want to sit in the chair; I wanted to stand behind it. My mother's persistence — her making a way out of no way — was the battery in my back. She was showing me, even then, what it meant to advocate for your kids, to get them in the door, to keep them looking like they mattered. That's one of the reasons I became a barber. Her love and that Big Alma grit run right through my clippers even now.

The Barbershop Village

~The invisible curriculum for life

The first barbershop I ever remember was a narrow storefront on 3rd Avenue, tucked between the Spanish church and Holy Tabernacle. Before it was Cameo's it was Heavy's; before Heavy's, something else. By the time my mother started bringing us there, it was a small, bright hole-in-the-wall where the waiting chairs lined one side like pews.

My very first barber was Sly — light-skinned, mustached, looking like George Jefferson with a steady hand. He sat in the second chair on the right, just after Heavy's station. Heavy himself, older and built like an old-school Rick Ross, anchored the shop. They were the first men to put clippers to my head. They had to hold me down; me and my brothers fed off each other's nerves, one crying harder if the other cried first.

Up Fulton Avenue was Jesse's Barbershop. Jesse Sr. eventually left it to his sons Jess and Jeff. Two young brothers cutting side by side, quiet but good, running the shop for years. Next door Santiago had his Puerto

Rican shop — Black barbers on one side, latino barbers on the other, no beef, no rivalry. The people with finer hair went to Santiago; the ones with coarse hair went to Jess and Jeff. The smell of pizza drifted up from the shop at the bottom of the hill.

Those were my classrooms. I watched Derrick and his cousin Darren — young barbers then, older than me but still close enough for me to imagine myself in their shoes. Darren with his sloped flat-top and blond streak, black leather Timberland chukkas and a Hawaiian shirt under his denim jumper. I remember asking about his boots and he explained to me that they were good to wear when you stand up all day. I thought he was the coolest man alive. Any time I played barbershop as a kid, I pretended to be Darren.

Cameo, cool and in his twenties, owned his own shop. Derrick and his cousin Darren started there and then moved on. Byo was Derrick's right hand. Moe Dread, Boo Black, Mr. Hoover at Cuts Galore — each of them left fingerprints on my craft. Emilio, elegant with the clippers, scissors with that downtown flare, taught me razors like a runway stylist. They showed me not just how to cut but how to carry yourself behind the chair.

And then there was Doobie. He was a little older than me — maybe ten years — already licensed, steady, and respected by everyone. Doobie handled his business without a trace of arrogance. He wasn't a pushover, but he was the nicest guy in the room, the one everyone liked. Cutting next to him, I asked a million questions. He answered every one. Watching him with his daughter Cheyenne showed me what fatherhood could look like behind the chair. She was only a year or two older than Dominae back then, and seeing the way he balanced cutting hair with raising a little girl gave me a blueprint. Doobie didn't know it, but he was helping me become the kind of father I am now. He showed me that you could be present, disciplined, and still gentle — a father in every sense while building your name as a barber.

Rest in peace to Ramadan, who managed New Africa. He's the one who gave me the keys, let me open and close, sweep and clean in exchange for keeping eighty percent of my earnings. That responsibility planted the first seed of ownership in my head. It's tragic that his life was cut short; he played a quiet but huge part in mine.

There were shop owners like Miki'al, who bought Cuts Galore and turned it into New Africa. Nuncie and Vanessa, two of the greatest beauticians you could ever meet. Charles, the African brother at International Barbershop who gave me another shot. Miguel on Burnside and Jerome. Darwin — one of the best barbers you'll ever see. Julio at Who's First and Who's Next on 149th. Chris "CI," Big Dog. Fern, who taught me the dry shave and how to "freeze" a line before hitting it with the straight razor. Manny from Morris Park.

And the ones I've poured into: Vinny, Nique (the baddest woman with clippers), our first apprentice Evel, my man Malik— born on my tenth birthday, a student of the game and of life, now thirty-four with a good head on his shoulders. Watching them grow has been as satisfying as any cut I've done.

And then there's Nay. He's more than a partner — he's my brother. We've been like Felix and Oscar at times, but through it all we've held each other down. He's the first person I truly connected with in the barber game, showing me college homecomings at Stony Brook when I didn't know anything about college, helping me see bigger possibilities and encouraging me to go to college. Without him there is no twenty-four-year-old me opening a barbershop. Without me there's no Nay making his moves. We've been in each other's weddings, each other's lives, each other's plans ever since. Six hundred miles apart and still collaborating, still dreaming, still building legacies. He is family.

I could go on. Some are still cutting, some have passed, some have moved on to other lives.
But each of them poured something into me, even the ones who didn't know I was watching. Because they

shared their craft with a kid, I can't not share mine now.

And above them all, my mother. Big Alma. She bragged about me from day one, even when we were broke. She is the spine of my art, the lavender running down every book I publish. Without her, I wouldn't be a barber, a poet, or a man with enough confidence to stand behind the chair and give back what was given to me.

I grew up inside a world that was bigger than four walls and mirrors. The shop was a village. Every barber, every clipper stroke, every piece of hair that hit the floor, every conversation in the waiting chairs carried a lesson. Some men knew they were teaching; most had no idea. Even those only a few years older than me were already veterans in the craft, and without realizing it they were silent instructors—showing me how to stand, how to speak, how to build a clientele, how to keep my dignity.

I watched the way they handled clippers and customers, the way they dressed, even the way they argued or stayed cool under pressure. Some of their missteps shaped me as much as their successes. Just like in any real village, you learn from the people who get it right and from the people who stumble. All of it sinks in. All of it shapes you.

I owe a quiet debt to the ones who thought nobody was watching. I was watching. I saw the examples you set. I learned how to be a barber, a businessman, and a man by studying your moves and your mistakes. And now, decades later, I'm pouring those same lessons into the young barbers and clients who sit in my chair.

The shop was never just a business for me; it's been a living classroom, a family room, at one point even a temporary home for me but most of all, it was a training ground for life. I came into the village as a kid with clippers, and now I'm one of its elders—cutting, guiding, and teaching in the same village that raised me.

From the lessons spoken and taught over clippers to the wisdom etched into my own hands, I look at who I've become and marvel at how far the village carried me.

Barbershop Griot

~Blending a Legacy, Sharpening Truths

In West Africa, a griot was more than a musician. He was a living library—poet, singer, historian, and keeper of the people's memory. In villages without books, the griot carried the archives in his voice. He recited family lineages, remembered victories and losses, turned news into song so that history survived in rhythm and rhyme. A griot didn't just tell stories; he safeguarded identity.

When I first learned that word, something clicked. My hands were already on clippers, but my heart was on history. A Black barber of West African descent—descended from people who survived ships, chains, and silence—cutting hair in America's South. My chair became my stage, my pulpit, my archive. Like the griots before me, I wasn't just shaping hair; I was shaping memory.

I've always been a storyteller. I sing lead for a rock band called Freezy and the Fades. I write poetry and children's books based on real kids and real neighborhoods. I stand onstage telling jokes, but my comedy is storytelling, not self-deprecation—colorful scenes you can see in your head. I study history for pleasure. I can remember what someone wore in 1987. I've found my family's slave schedules and census records. My relatives call me the family historian. This isn't just a hobby; it's who I am.

In the barbershop, those instincts find their home. Every cut comes with a story. Clients share deployments, custody battles, first dates, and funerals. Soldiers from Fort Bragg sit where hustlers once sat. Kids who watched me cut their fathers' hair now bring their own sons. I listen, remember, and pass on what's worth keeping—lessons, warnings, jokes, prayers— like a modern-day griot with clippers instead of a kora.

I didn't plan to become this. One day I was a kid sneaking peeks at the older barbers honing their craft, and then I blinked and I was the one holding the stories. By nature and by trade, I've become a Barbershop Griot—blending a legacy, sharpening truths—keeping our history alive one cut, one conversation, one memory at a time.

ACKNOWLEDGMENTS

This book isn't mine alone. It's a collection of memories, lessons, and blessings I've been given over decades. I'm not just the storyteller — I'm a recipient of the experience, passing it on like a griot without a quota.

First, I thank the barbers and ancestors who came before me. Black barbers were some of the first Black entrepreneurs, building an industry where independence and dignity went hand in hand. You laid the foundation we stand on.

Mr. Hoover — you gave a 14-year-old kid a chance to watch, learn, and then cut in your shop. That chance turned into a career, a calling, and a lifetime of purpose. Kool-Aid, thank you for believing in me too. Darren Kelly, you probably don't even know who I am, but as a kid I watched your skill, posture, and manners and said, "I'm going to be like him." That spark still burns.

Derrick Kelly, Byo — you showed me what it meant to be young, fresh, witty, and talented in the game. Derrick, your resilience after your health battle is an inspiration. Boo Black, rest in peace. Ramadan, thank you for making my load lighter and planting the seed of ownership. Doobie, one of the most genuine people you'll ever meet — your example of fatherhood and leadership stays with me. Charnay (Nay), my partner and brother — we've shared visions and built them together from day one. Moe Dread, thank you for your humility and generosity.

To all the others — my boy Darwin, Julio Berringer, Chris "CI," Fernando "Fern" Ithier, Manny Manuel, Nuncie and Vanessa,

269

Charles — each of you poured something into me. Whether you know it or not, you helped shape my craft and my character.

To my clients — you're the heartbeat of this work. NYPD brothers like Andre Mazyck (rest in peace), Lee Green (rest in peace), Tracy Travis, Mike McPhee, Rashaun Austin, Alfred "Smitty" Smith. Clients like Oz Johnson and Tim Johnson, Brandon Taliferro, Omar Petty, Wendell Clark, Tone who keep the barbershop spirit alive. Chris Crawford, my first friend and first client in North Carolina — I've watched your son Ethan grow up in my chair from age 5 to college. If I forgot your name here, please know I haven't forgotten your impact.

To my mom, Alma Mae Mack — Big Alma. You are the spine of my art, the lavender thread through every page. You believed in me, bragged about me, and sacrificed for me. Rest in peace. To my brothers Milton and Joshua — my first guinea pigs and first believers.

My NC barbers Vinnie McNeil, Edgar Thomas (Rest in Peace) Niq the Barber Doll, love you guys. Keep the industry lit and keep doing it the right way.

Finally, to all barbers past, present, and future: keep the dignity, respect, and integrity of the shop alive. It's more than a business. It's a sanctuary, a training ground, and a safe space for our burdens. Listen, learn, and one day you'll be that OG, that griot, passing on not just a skill but a culture.

Peace,
Freezy the Barber

ABOUT THE AUTHOR

James A. Freeman, professionally known as "Freezy the Barber," is a Bronx-born master barber and storyteller who has spent more than three decades shaping both hairlines and narratives. Cutting since the age of fourteen, he discovered that the barbershop is more than a business — it's a classroom, a sanctuary, and a stage where everyday lives and hidden histories unfold.

He began his publishing journey with acclaimed children's titles, including the beloved holiday book A Sweet Potato Pie for Santa and I, That Is Not My Name, the forthcoming early chapter-book series The Thought Bubble, and Angalia Juu, which features his daughter Journey and introduces young readers to Swahili. He has also contributed to and published other authors' work through his independent imprint, Washington Avenue Press.

Painting With Words marked Freeman's debut adult literary work. Faded Into Truth is his second — a continuation of his mission to preserve memories, lessons, and voices from behind the chair and beyond it. Today he channels that same energy into mentoring barbers and authors alike, proving that the chair can be a stage, a classroom, and a bridge between lives

He is the founder and Executive Publisher of Washington Avenue Press, an independent publishing house dedicated to amplifying community voices—"where culture, craft, and community converge." Through this platform, Freeman mentors emerging authors and brings underrepresented stories into print.

www.ingramcontent.com/pod-product-compliance
Lightning Source LLC
Chambersburg PA
CBHW060128130626
46556CB00006B/2271